W9-DHL-368

New Stone Technology, Design, and Construction for Exterior Wall Systems

Barry Donaldson, editor

Special Technical Publication (STP) 996

1916 Race Street, Philadelphia, PA 19103

Library of Congress Cataloging-in-Publication Data

New stone technology, design, and construction for exterior wall systems/Barry Donaldson, editor.

(ASTM special technical publication; 996)
"Papers presented at the Exterior Stone Symposium 1987, which was held in New York City on 12 March 1987 . . . sponsored by ASTM Committee C18 on Natural Building Stones . . . [et al.]"—Foreword.
Includes bibliographies and indexes.
"ASTM publication code number (PCN) 04-996000-10."
ISBN 0-8031-1164-9
1. Building, Stone.   2. Exterior walls.   3. Facades.
I. Donaldson, Barry.   II. American Society for Testing and Materials.   III. Exterior Stone Symposium 1987 (1987: New York, NY)   IV. ASTM Committee C18 on Natural Building Stones.
V. Series.
   TH1201.N4   1988   693'.1—dc19   88-2358

Copyright © by AMERICAN SOCIETY FOR TESTING AND MATERIALS 1988

NOTE

The Society is not responsible, as a body,
for the statements and opinions
advanced in this publication.

Peer Review Policy

Each paper published in this volume was evaluated by three peer reviewers. The authors addressed all of the reviewers' comments to the satisfaction of both the technical editor(s) and the ASTM Committee on Publications.

The quality of the papers in this publication reflects not only the obvious efforts of the authors and the technical editor(s), but also the work of these peer reviewers. The ASTM Committee on Publications acknowledges with appreciation their dedication and contribution of time and effort on behalf of ASTM.

Printed in Baltimore
March 1988

Foreword

This publication, *New Stone Technology, Design, and Construction for Exterior Wall Systems, ASTM STP 996,* contains papers presented at the Exterior Stone Symposium 1987, which was held in New York City on 12 March 1987. The symposium was sponsored by ASTM Committee C18 on Natural Building Stones, ASTM Committee E6 on Performance of Building Constructions, Tishman Research Corp., Internazionale Marmi e Macchine Carrara, and McGraw-Hill Publications. Barry Donaldson, Tishman Research Corp., served as editor of this publication.

Acknowledgments

The following benefactors have generously provided support for the symposium upon which this book is based:

Artex Precast Ltd.
P.O. Box 149 LAK 1B2
Concord, Ontario CAN

Cygnus Panel Systems
1580 Lincoln
Number 1200
Denver, Colorado 80203

Dow Corning Corp.
3901 S. Saginaw Rd.
Midland, Michigan 48686

Euromarble S.p.a.
Via Provincaile 160
54031 Carrara, Avenza, Italy

F.E.I. Limited Inc.
One River Street
Building 72A
Hastings-on-Hudson,
NY 10706

Henraux S.p.a.
Querceta—Lucca, Italy

International Quarries
A Div. of Ital-Fintex Corporation
9411 Wallisville Road
Houston, TX 77013

Laticrete International, Inc.
1 Laticrete Park North
Bethany, CT 06525-3498

PPG Industries
One PPG Place
Pittsburgh, PA

Testwell Craig Labs Italy
Via Capriglia
Al Logo
Pietrasanta, Lucca, Italy

Testwell Craig Berger Inc.
36-20 13th Street
Long Island City, NY 11106

Vistawall Architectural Products
P.O. Box 629
803 Airport Road
Terrell, TX 75160

Contents

Overview

Today there is a strong emphasis on architectural eclecticism combined with technological innovation, and its expression is especially clear in the design and technology of stone facades. Curtain-wall structures continue to become much lighter and faster to install, and stone as a material unequalled for durability, richness, and color is replacing the minimal glass curtain-wall designs so popular during the 1960s and 1970s. The growth of new building methods and the renewed interest in the use of natural stone have led to many innovations in the way stone may be applied to the exterior of buildings. Numerous developments have occurred at such a rapid pace that there has been little information available for a better understanding of many new systems.

The application of today's most sophisticated building technologies to an age-old material such as stone poses many concerns about the quality and durability that had never existed before. The use of thin stone veneers on large, tall buildings in harsh climates and conditions imposes the need for close scrutiny and control throughout every step of the building process.

Recent developments in cutting and fabricating techniques allow the use of thin lightweight stone veneers supported by steel truss frames, precast concrete panels, glass fiber–reinforced cement (GFRC) panels, aluminum "stick frames," or diaphragm panel systems. In addition, the application of latex portland cements, structural silicones, and polymer gaskets to stone veneers is providing new opportunities for the fabrication of lightweight panel systems. The result is the availability of systems that are lighter, more economical, and faster to erect than conventionally anchored stone. Integration of various building components, reduction of labor-intensive hand setting, and acceleration of construction schedules have promoted greater use of stone even at a time when skilled stonemasons are fewer and construction costs higher than ever before.

Thin stone veneers are now available as a result of sophisticated fabrication equipment that uses laser-guided and computer-controlled diamond circular saws and gang saws which cut stone with less vibration and very close tolerances. This technology makes veneers available from 1 1/2 in. to less than 3/8 in. in thickness. Although thinner veneers mean greater economy, the stone specified for a building facade becomes structurally critical when used in veneers of 1 1/4 in. or less in thickness. Cutting kerfs for clip or disk anchors and drilling holes for blind-pin anchors or spring clips are much more difficult with thin stone, and especially with stone that has a great deal of veining or physical impurities that will affect its strength, or stone that has a crystalline structure with dimensions large enough to approach the thickness of the slab itself and therefore substantially weaken it.

Not surprisingly, a great deal of controversy has grown around the use of exterior stone veneers 1 1/4 in. and less in thickness. The concern is that there is neither sufficient evidence of the long-term durability of such veneers nor standard test procedures for measuring stone strength, especially in terms of flexure and modulus of rupture. Furthermore, international cooperation to support the sharing of information on stone availability and performance is inadequate. With the growing use of thin stone veneers, strength characteristics, factors of safety, design tolerances, and quality of workmanship have become much more critical to ensuring the durability of the system.

Many new stone systems involve fabrication of a number of individual stone slabs into larger panels that are attached to the building structure. Panelization allows for faster building enclosure and acceleration of the start time for interior trades, but requires that repetition of wall elements (spandrel panels, window panels, column covers, etc.) be distributed over a large enough volume to offset the costs of machining, formwork, or transportation associated with panel fabrication.

The Exterior Stone Symposium 1987 was organized with the objective of providing a forum for individuals with extensive experience in the use of new stone materials and methods for exterior walls to share their knowledge. The symposium focused on the experiences of architects, engineers, producers, and fabricators as illustrated by case studies of different projects. The presentations addressed specific building projects and described recommendations to insure good design and construction. Actual building projects were used to illustrate a history of performance in terms of the quality and durability of many systems or the deterioration and failure of other systems. Describing the successes and failures of different designs provides a valuable resource for designers, fabricators, and erectors. By emphasizing the application of stone in the context of total systems, it is possible to understand the relationship between different building disciplines (architects, engineers, fabricators, etc.) and their effect on the quality of the overall design. The one-day event covered topics such as analysis and testing of stone, design criteria, and discussions of different exterior wall systems such as truss-supported panels, precast and fiber glass–reinforced cement panels, adhered thin stone veneers, and curtain wall-framed systems.

The results of the symposium are intended to be useful to architects, structural engineers, fabricators, erectors, and standards organizations. Design details and performance characteristics are described for a variety of systems, different methods of fabrication are illustrated, and the advantages and disadvantages of different erection techniques are described.

Throughout the presentations there are references to the use of current standards as well as recommendations for further development of standards. Many of the overall conclusions and recommendations of the symposium are summarized below:

1. Develop design guidelines and details for thin stone veneer exterior wall systems. These guidelines and details should distinguish between different stone types and different panelization techniques.

2. Define appropriate design tolerances for thin stone veneer exterior wall systems including dimensional tolerances, anticipated movement due to moisture and temperature, joint treatment and size, panel span capabilities, deflection limits, bowing, and racking.

3. Develop test procedures which are more representative of actual conditions such as dimension, finish, and system performance. Tests for determining compressive strength, flexural strength, and modulus of rupture are defined by ASTM but may require modification to reflect actual stone thicknesses and finishes for a particular job.

4. Establish the actual range of physical characteristics for different types of stone and determine whether the mean or lower values should be used as the basis for specifications. Such a procedure would require defining standard sampling methods and commonly accepted safety factors.

5. Integrate the design guidelines and recommendations of different organizations representing exterior wall systems into common language and criteria.

6. Develop a method for the inventory and tracking of stone from the quarry to the site. The purpose of this is to be able to relate the performance of individual stone slabs to its specific source in the quarry.

7. Develop long-term weather testing procedures, especially as it relates to the performance of adhered systems and to the performance of these veneers under conditions of extreme freeze, thaw, and corrosive environments.

8. Initiate greater international cooperation between stone-producing countries to develop common language, format, and content for standards.

This symposium is the first in a series of lecture programs on new technology, design, and construction. Future programs will continue to focus on areas of innovation and controversy and where there is a clear need for more information. Also, there will be a continued emphasis on the experiences derived from actual building projects and from an understanding of the overall performance of building systems.

This symposium would not have been possible without the many individuals, companies, and institutions who contributed their financial and personal support toward its success. For their support, a special recognition is given to Artex Precast Ltd., Cygnus Panel Systems, Dow Corning Corp., Euromarble S.P.A., F.E.I. Ltd., Henreaux S.P.A., International Quarries, Latricrete International Inc., PPG Industries, Testwell Craig Labs Italy, Testwell Craig Berger Inc., and Vistawall Architecture Products.

In addition, many individuals gave enormous amounts of time and energy toward the Exterior Stone Symposium 1987. Many thanks to each and all of the friends and colleagues who were a part of this event. To Roberto Meini, Alberto Ricci, and Francesca Lofaro, who were enormously helpful in bringing our friends to join us from Italy. To Marco Tonelli, who was one of our greatest supporters from Italy. To Darl Rastorfer, who understood better than anyone the need to get more technical information out to the building community. To Michelle Albert, who handled all of the public relations and communications for the symposium. To Rose Saggio, for her patience and continued support on the computer. To Jinette Quinones, whose organizational skill, tireless efforts, and invaluable assistance kept the program running smoothly, and to Joseph Newman, whose leadership and guidance will always remain a source of inspiration, direction, and a great deal of fun.

Barry Donaldson
Tishman Research Corp., New York, NY
10103; symposium chairman and editor

Introduction

Opening remarks at the Exterior Stone Symposium, 12 March 1987, McGraw-Hill Auditorium, New York, New York.

A hearty welcome to the more than 500 members of the building community from near and far who have joined us today at this forum. I hasten to apologize to the more than 200 people who we had to turn away. This unprecedented demand tells me that what we suspected was true, namely, that holding this Exterior Stone Symposium was worthwhile.

This is the first such symposium addressing the actual experiences of architects, engineers, producers, and fabricators not only with regard to the individual aspects of stone technology but with respect to the total system. This symposium is unique not only because all the players are involved, but because they have come together with the realization that the best results occur when there is team cooperation and sharing of experience.

This symposium is unique because it examines developments that have occurred in a recent short span of ten years—a span of time when use of stone for exterior walls grew at such a rapid pace that there has not been an opportunity before this to review, assess, discuss, and summarize what has happened technologically.

This symposium is unique because of its four-party sponsorship: Tishman Research, the technological arm of a user and construction manager who has a proven record of introducing worthwhile new building technology; ASTM, the nationally recognized leader in promulgating voluntary consensus standards; Internazionale Marmi e Macchine Carrara, the Italian stone association with foremost knowledge in production and technology; and McGraw-Hill, renowned worldwide for its dissemination of technical and business information.

I would like to thank each of the sponsors as well as the benefactors who have made this symposium possible. I also wish to thank the speakers, moderators, and others working behind the scenes.

I would now like to set the tone for this meeting with a few comments. We are now witnessing a new age of buildings because buildings are better places in which to work, live, and interact. They are more durable, better designed, easier to maintain, and utilize higher quality materials and products. In this new age of buildings, owners are setting higher standards for the built environment and demand more value for this investment. Owners influence the final result more than ever before.

In this new age of buildings the emphasis is not only on improving productivity of the activities that take place within buildings but on giving more attention to alternatives and style. It is the era of better materials and improved design which I refer to as the "era of higher expectation." This has helped the growth of the use of stone.

To help decisionmakers make choices there is more information readily available than ever before by voice, video, in print, and by computer, enabling the decisionmaker to be more knowledgeable about what's available and what's possible. This exposure to the rich variety of available alternatives feeds the expectation level of the decisionmaker. I hope this symposium enhances this exposure and that the Italian and U.S. stone industries will develop adequate and useful information on a continuing basis, and that the spirit of international cooperation, evidenced here today, will grow.

We are also in an era of increasing individuality. This leads to more customization of product and service to meet the specific needs of users. Historically, as mass production grew, flexibility and freedom of choice were largely lost. Machines and assembly lines vastly improved speed and quality, but at the expense of much reduced flexibility. Economies of the past were economies of scale, and it just wasn't possible to make a fewer number of units of a specialized design at a reasonable cost. The challenge is to restore flexibility, and I believe that the stone industry has met this challenge in large part because they recognized the trend towards specialty custom high performance and upscale products and services, and understood that the decisionmaker is willing to trade bottom line dollars—particularly where it can improve his business—for individuality and freedom of choice. I am sure that each of you has your own views on individuality—but you can't escape the fact that today's and tomorrow's decisionmakers listen to a different drummer than yesterday's pacesetters.

Yes, today's goods and services cost more because we expect them to do more and, for the most part, users and consumers receive more value. They may fight to get the lowest price, but the auction is at a higher dollar level.

In the new age of buildings, there is a growing concern about improving maintainability and operation of buildings. This bodes well for the stone industry.

Decisionmakers want to know levels of quality available, price ranges, and expected performance. The owner's new desire to see a broader picture and to consider new alternatives, in my judgment, provides new opportunities that insure that technological progress will continue.

The time has come to recognize that, unlike many of the technological evolutions of the past, there is no single rallying point. Today, progress requires the involvement of more professionals, decisionmakers, and contractors than ever before. Therefore, bringing together the diverse interests, as we are doing today, to learn from one another—to make good things happen—makes good sense.

If the diverse interests in the building community cooperate and think more positively, more broadly, they can shape change more readily and for everyone's benefit.

I hope you will find this conference beneficial and take the opportunity to get to know one another better.

Thank you for coming, and, once again, welcome to Exterior Stone Symposium—1987, and to New York City . . . where as they say, "if you can make it here, you can make it anywhere."

Joseph H. Newman
President, Tishman Research Corp.,
New York, NY

Analysis and Testing of Stone

Irwin G. Cantor[1] and Mary Beth Juda

The New Stone Age: Overcoming the Structural Stumbling Blocks

REFERENCE: Cantor, I. G. and Juda, M. B., **"The New Stone Age: Overcoming the Structural Stumbling Blocks,"** *New Stone Technology, Design, and Construction for Exterior Wall Systems, ASTM STP 996*, B. Donaldson, Ed., American Society for Testing and Materials, Philadelphia, 1988, pp. 3–10.

ABSTRACT: Structural aspects of stone cladding systems are described and compared. Conventional set stone, curtain wall, and backup truss systems are investigated schematically, with examples illustrating solutions to the structural problems of differential and lateral building movement in addition to the details of stone attachment. Systems differ in means of accommodation and tolerance of structure and/or cladding movement, resulting in various influences on structural design. System type and stone strength are major factors determining the adequacy of the design of stone attachment details. Comprehensive stone testing is recommended due to the variability of the material and the lack of applicable standards for the thinner stones currently in use. A testing program using standard tests and project-based modifications is described which aides the engineer in interpreting the data for the particular stone and system type under investigation. The interaction between structure and stone cladding system requires structural solutions (based on stone testing) engineered to efficiently and economically address the design's requirements.

KEY WORDS: cladding, curtain wall, stone facings, stone attachments

Recent trends in architecture include a growth in the use of granite and marble facades in high-rise structures. The increased use of stone cladding is due not only to an interest in the aesthetic qualities of the materials, but is also a result of the new technology. New attachment systems enable these materials to enhance the clean, sleek line of contemporary structures. These technical developments have led to the use of thinner stones (30 mm), demanding a more thorough investigation of the cladding and the attachment system to ensure their structural safety.

The kind of cladding system used on a particular building is determined by a number of factors, including the economic, structural, and architectural aspects of the project. Three of the many possible systems are: conventional set stone applied to backup masonry, stone in a glazed or curtain wall system, and stone applied to prefabricated backup trusses. The type of system chosen affects and is affected by both the stone and the structure. The interrelation of these three components, stone, system, and structure, points to the need for close engineering involvement from the beginning of the project.

In the conventional system the stone is attached to the masonry with holding clips and the masonry is supported by the structural framework. In the glazed-in system, stone panels are slipped into recesses in a conventional mullion stick system and held in place by gasketing, very similar to a glazed window system. Another and similar approach is to secure the stone with continuous or partial length angles set into kerfs in the stone. The stone truss system

---

[1] Chief executive officer, Office of Irwin G. Cantor PC, New York, NY 10017.

creates larger units of stone panels usually spanning horizontally from column to column, thus applying no gravity loadings to the structure's spandrel beams.

When comparing either the glazed-in or the truss system to a conventional approach, it is clear that a significant advantage is weight. The masonry backup system can easily weigh two or three times that of either of the other systems. If the masonry backup wall is not a part of the central support system of the building, this load is transmitted to the building frame without return or benefit of any kind. The impact of this additional weight is even more significant in buildings located in earthquake-prone zones where the structure must be further stiffened to carry this dead load.

Structurally, the first area of concern is the method of supporting the system on the building. The key factor is to insure that building movement is recognized and that allowances in connections, granite joints, caulking sizing, etc. are made to prevent disturbing the cladding. However, the effect of the cladding and its supporting system upon the structure must also be considered.

Figures 1 and 2 schematically represent the methods of support of the typical mullion and truss systems.

The curtain wall for the E. F. Hutton office building, a 28-story, 600 000-ft² structure in New York City, is comprised of a stick system with two-story-high mullions. Each mullion is attached to the structure via a yoke anchor and insert plate at two different floor levels. The top connection for each mullion is a fixed anchor which must resist dead load as well as wind load. The lower connection is an expansion anchor which resists only wind load in the lateral direction. This connection allows longitudinal displacement to accommodate the effects of thermal expansion and prevent the imposition of loads due to building motion under wind or live load.

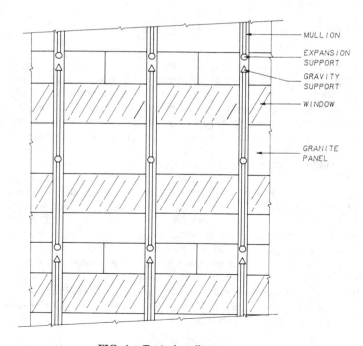

MULLION

EXPANSION SUPPORT

GRAVITY SUPPORT

WINDOW

GRANITE PANEL

FIG. 1—*Typical mullion system.*

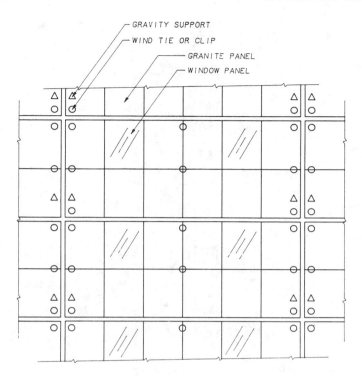

FIG. 2—*Typical truss system.*

The inserts consist of steel plates embedded in the edge of the building's floor slab at regular intervals. The plates have slotted holes to allow for construction tolerances. The plates provide a surface for connecting the curtain wall anchors and mullions to the main structure. Between mullions, each granite panel is held top and bottom by extruded aluminum anchors in continuous kerfs. A typical connection detail is shown in Fig. 3.

At the 7 World Trade Center site, the stone trusses used most frequently span from column to column for the height of one story. Each truss may be considered in two parts. The bottom section of the truss, the spandrel portion, supports the upper portion, consisting of windows or windows framed with granite insets. The spandrel section is supported on the column at each end by a gravity anchor. One end of the truss is rigidly attached while the other end is allowed to move horizontally by the use of slotted holes and Teflon pads. In addition to the gravity anchor at each end, the truss is attached to the structure with several wind ties which connect it to the column, floor slab, or spandrel beam. Figure 4 represents a typical connection.

In any cladding system, the effect of the attachments upon the structure must be accounted for in the design process. Connections must be designed to transfer the effects of any eccentricities to the structure. Spandrel beams and slabs must be checked for rotation or horizontal deflection if they are used as the cladding support members. These constraints apply regardless of the type of system employed.

An important difference between the two systems occurs in the accommodation of movements of structure and/or cladding. The glazed-in system allows individual stone panel movement, whereas the truss system relies upon one "fixed" point for each truss with the

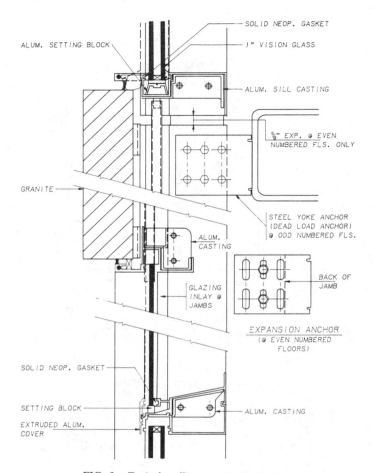

FIG. 3—*Typical mullion connection detail.*

wind ties and expansion anchor allowing for differential structural movement. The truss system is the more unforgiving of the two systems in that its components are larger. Therefore, the same building movement has a greater impact over the area of the component.

Because the truss system typically spans and is supported on the exterior columns of the building, the placement of these columns is a major consideration in evaluating the suitability of the truss solution over the mullion system. If the columns are too close together, many short trusses may be required unless alternate columns are used as supports. A more limiting situation occurs when the columns are spaced too far apart. Transportation and handling may be a problem if the truss becomes disproportionately long. A solution to this problem is the development of connection details which allow one end of the truss to rest on the structure's spandrel beams. In this case it is crucial to insure that deflections fall within acceptable limits or truss joints can vary sharply in thickness.

The second area of concern in the design of the cladding system is the method of stone attachment. Here the choice of system and the strength of the stone are closely linked in determining the adequacy of the design. The major consideration is the ability of the stone to span between the supports provided by the system. In the conventional granite on backup

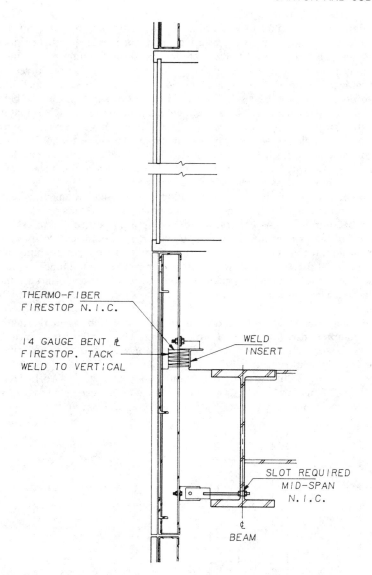

FIG. 4—*Typical truss system connection between columns.*

system, the stone must be checked to see that it can resist the stresses in suction and pressure developed when spanning between the holding clips. In the glazed-in system, the stone must be checked for spanning between mullions. In both of these systems, if the stone cannot span, the thickness may have to be increased. In the truss system, more control is available since additional pins can be added to tie the stone to the backup truss, if the stone strength is inadequate at the desired thickness or if the span is too great.

Particular attention must be paid to the problem of attaching the stone to the truss with stainless steel pins held in with epoxy. One governmental agency has a concern that epoxy may deteriorate over a number of years or be totally destroyed in a fire and therefore be unable to hold the stone. A mechanical attachment must consequently be added to the design. The pin cannot be placed horizontally or the stone (assuming total failure of the epoxy and only nominal friction) would fall under negative or suction forces. After testing models with the pin bent and the holes filled with plaster of paris which has no bond strength, we determined the best solution would be to "hickey" the pin up between 12.5 and 22.5° as shown in the detail of Fig. 5. The advantage of the 12.5° angle is that it increases the tensile strength in the pullout since the "heel" does not get impacted as much as it would with a 22.5° angle. However, the mechanical anchorage of the 22.5° angle is better since it becomes more difficult for the stone to "ride up and out" under negative pressure than with a 12.5°. We call for a complete round of tests in tension and shear on the stone anchorage to insure that it meets the design requirements.

Finally, and most importantly, the type of cladding stone used has an overwhelming effect on the system development. The thinness of stone now in use presents problems which have never before been an issue. As previously, the strength properties (compression, tension, and shear) are of major concern. Currently, however, the coefficients of the thermal and moisture expansion, the effects of repeated temperature variation, permeability of the stone, and the durability and resistance to weathering bear increasing influence as the thickness of stone used decreases. Other physical characteristics which become more important are the size of grain, overall quality, and variability of the specific type of stone to be used on the project.

Due to the lack of available standards and the natural variability of the material itself, we advise a comprehensive program of stone testing. The standard tests historically performed to check stone quality are the ASTM tests for absorption, compressive strength, abrasion, and modulus of rupture.

The value of testing is illustrated by one of our major projects—7 World Trade Center. This 185 000 m² (1.8 million ft²), 47-story complex includes a facade clad in 3.2 ha (8 acres) of both polished and thermally treated Carmen Red granite from Finland.

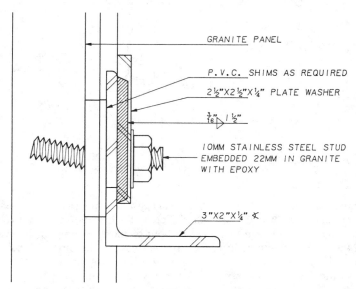

GRANITE PANEL

P.V.C. SHIMS AS REQUIRED

2½"X2½"X¼" PLATE WASHER

$\frac{3}{16}$" 1½"

10MM STAINLESS STEEL STUD EMBEDDED 22MM IN GRANITE WITH EPOXY

3"X2"X¼" ✗

FIG. 5—*Stone attachment to truss.*

Testing various-sized granite stone under uniform loads determined the actual method of failure and strength of stone. Specially constructed water boxes were fabricated and samples tested to destruction. Results showed significant variation between ASTM C 99— modulus of rupture testing requirements—and the testing using actual stone thicknesses. ASTM Test Method for Modulus of Rupture of Natural Building Stone (C 99) tests are 101.6 by 203.2 by 57.2 mm (4 by 8 by 2 1/4 in.). The test samples were project sized at 101.6 by 203.2 by 30 mm (4 in. by 8 in. by 30 mm). In most instances the thin samples tested for rupture showed much *lower* strengths than predicted by C 99 formulas. A comparison of our results with those of ASTM C 880 flexure test results proved more realistic, although any large mineral inclusions can dramatically affect the findings from C 880 (Test Method for Flexural Strength of Natural Building) since the specimen is only 38 mm (1 1/2 in.) wide.

Based on these preliminary tests, we instituted a comprehensive examination program sampling from every fifth block in accordance with C 99 for modulus of rupture but modifying the specimen thickness to the actual slab thickness. Samples were also tested in true flexure spanning 96.5 mm (3 ft, 2 in.) between supports. A complete history was kept on each block. Weaker blocks and slabs were segregated from the satisfactory slabs and designated to be in panels placed in zones of less intense wind pressures or used in nonstructural modes such as pavers, coping stones, etc.

The Office of Irwin G. Cantor (OIGC) quickly realized the necessity of testing flamed as well as polished blocks. The flaming process "shocks" the stone and can damage between 2 and 3 mm of the surface, thus reducing the effective section available and seriously affecting the stone's performance relative to structural capacity.

Accelerated aging tests have been added to the battery of tests performed on stone samples. After cyclical heating and freezing of the specimens, they are tested to determine the modulus of elasticity.

Much engineering judgment must be used in interpreting test data and applying it to the situation at hand because of the lack of a long history in using granite in this manner. In an attempt to garner the most complete set of data on stone used on a recent project, 60 Wall Street, we called for "a minimum of 12 specimens divided into four groups: wet, dry, parallel to rift, and perpendicular to rift." It was discovered, however, that the rift for the Gris Mondari stone cladding for this project is not easily determined. The lowest value of strength from testing in either direction was consequently used as a basis for design.

In an effort to balance the inconsistencies of dealing with stone, the customary procedure has been to ask for a safety factor of 4. There is a movement now to reduce the safety factor to as low as 2 1/2 as we learn more about the characteristics of the stones and as the testing and inspection provided introduces quality controls which did not previously exist. We believe that the 10.34 MPa (1500 psi) called for in ASTM Specification for Granite Building Stone (C 615) is not sacrosanct as long as the actual strengths of the stone based upon testing are sufficient to satisfy the structural needs of the chosen system. With our comprehensive testing program, we are more than able to justify this conclusion.

The architectural and structural aspects of the project can be accommodated by a number of different solutions, although some are more suitable than others. The architectural design of the building may inherently determine the type of cladding system used. A design which accents the vertical lines of the structure is more readily achieved by the use of the glazed-in or stick mullion system. In contrast, a design with horizontal accentuation, such as one featuring strip windows, lends itself excellently to the truss system.

Some projects can utilize both mullion and truss solutions together, although an additional problem of coordination between the two system vendors must be recognized. Such a combination solution is being used on Logan Square Two in Philadelphia. However, the owner has insisted upon a single source of responsibility for the entire curtain wall.

In the final analysis, the selection of cladding system employed is based upon economics. The relationship between stone, system, and structure must solve the problems of differential movement while economically providing the architect with the desired appearance. Structural aspects must be reviewed early on in the design of the system so that the solution will efficiently address the particular problems encountered. Criteria for the stone testing program must be established by the architect/engineer early enough (and implemented during design) to insure that the stone thickness selected is adequate based upon the properties of a representative number of stone samples from an area of the quarry to be used for the project. In conclusion, each system has its advantages but also carries constraints which must be considered in the selection and final design of the project.

S. A. Bortz,[1] B. Erlin,[1] and C. B. Monk, Jr.[1]

Some Field Problems with Thin Veneer Building Stones

REFERENCE: Bortz, S. A., Erlin, B., and Monk, C. B., Jr., **"Some Field Problems with Thin Veneer Building Stones,"** *New Stone Technology, Design, and Construction for Exterior Wall Systems, ASTM STP 996*, B. Donaldson, Ed., American Society for Testing and Materials, Philadelphia, 1988, pp. 11–31.

ABSTRACT: The authors, in examining experiences with over 40 stone veneer buildings over the past decade, describe typical problems that have arisen in the use of limestone, travertine, marble, and granite.

The modern trend to thinner ornamental dimensional stone has resulted in the use of thicknesses down to 2 to 3 cm (7/8 to 1 3/16 in.)—a significant reduction from 5.08 to 7.62 cm (2 to 3 in.) that was regarded as a lower practical limit less than ten years ago. The authors examine the consequences of such thin stone veneer in terms of strength, durability, and architectural engineering performance. Material geology, quarrying and fabrication limitations, and environmental factors are considered.

Specific field problems encountered have included a variety of structural, architectural, petrographic, and erection problems. Structural problems have included torsional twisting or thin deep beam participation at spandrel beam locations. Architectural problems have embraced differential movement or water permeability issues that affect expansion joints of internal drainage systems. Petrographic work has examined the bowing of thin marble or the weathering of travertine. Erection has involved workmanship issues (including plant fabrication considerations) or field material handling and attachment techniques.

The authors conclude with a recommended list of design criteria to avoid future problems of the kind they have encountered.

KEY WORDS: thin stone veneers, limestone, travertine, marble, granite, prefabricated stone systems, thin stone anchorage problems, thin stone workmanship problems, thin stone material and design problems

The authors, in examining experience with over 40 distressed stone veneer buildings over the past decade, describe typical problems that have arisen in the use of limestone, travertine, marble, and granite. While some of the buildings were built before 1960, the majority have been constructed during the last 25 years and many within the last decade. The stone facades being considered are less than 5 cm thick. Typically they may range downward in thickness as follows: 5 cm (1 15/16 in.); 4 cm (1 9/16 in.); 3 cm (1 3/16 in.); 2.5 cm (1 in.); and 2.0 cm (13/16 in.). The maximum size stone is generally not over 20 ft² (1.86 m², giving rise to the following typical sizes (expressed in feet): 4 by 5 (1.22 by 1.52 m); 3 by 6 2/3 (0.92 by 2.03 m); 2 1/2 by 8 (0.76 by 2.44 m); 2 by 10 (0.61 by 3.05 m).

Traditional stone quarrying and fabrication techniques control these limits. The weight of such stones is generally under 600 lb (1320 kg) each—down to where two or four men can handle the piece. However, when combined into prefabricated assemblies, the weights

[1] Senior consultant, principal, and senior consultant, respectively, Wiss, Janney, Elstner Associates, Inc., Northbrook, IL 60062.

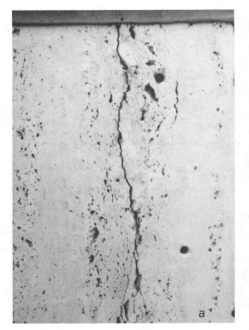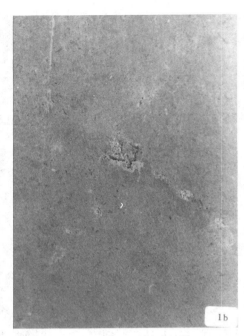

FIG. 1—*Possible weathering sites in stone veneer:* (a) *travertine crazing;* (b) *marble or limestone veining.*

FIG. 2—*Permanent residual deflection in stone veneer systems:* (a) *marble bowing;* (b) *curling of precast panels.*

FIG. 3—*Views of a large mineral grain greater than 1/10 the stone thickness:* (a) *pyroxine granite;* (b) *biotite* (*mica*) *granite.*

can rise from one to five tons (0.91 to 4.54 metric tons), where the reach of a crane may control the size lifted. Prefabricated may include either support directly on a metal grid system or cast on to the surface of precast concrete panels.

This paper examines typical field problems that have been encountered in the investigations of the authors. These, for convenience, have been subdivided into the following categories:

1. Material problems.
2. Design problems.
3. Anchorage problems.
4. Workmanship problems.

Necessarily, there is an overlap between such arbitrary separate categories. Any given field case is frequently a combination. A frequently encountered category is workmanship. This may be due to the fact that before the advent of high-rise thin veneer facades, such veneers were primarily utilized in building interiors: lobbies, hallways, and large rooms of monumental educational, cultural, medical, religious, civic, or commercial spaces. Utilizing hand-twisted copper wires, blind mortar anchor pockets, and plaster of paris spotting mortar, a traditional satisfactory hand-fastening methodology was developed for such interior use. With the advent of thin veneer *exterior* use, this same technique was initially applied with minimum regard to more severe exterior weather exposure, increased lateral wind loading, and greater differential movements due to thermal and moisture changes.

As one traces the stone veneer anchorage shown in *Architectural Graphic Standards* (from 1932, first edition, to 1981, seventh edition), earlier traditional interior wainscot techniques

FIG. 4—*Flame treatment of granite surfaces:* (a) *flame-treated granite surfaces to enhance color hue;* (b) *modulus of rupture testing.*

changed to more positive means of mechanical anchorage for exterior applications. Beginning with the sixth edition (1970), twisted wire anchorage was limited primarily to interior use. Better mechanical anchorage culminated with the appearance of metal grid systems in the seventh edition (1981). As will be shown, field installation practices were slow in adopting these anchorage standards.

Material Problems

With the advent of exterior thin stone veneer, weathering deterioration is more critical. Planes of weather weakness may exist along the veins in metamorphic marble stone and in the open texture of travertine, a sedementary limestone. Clay slip planes in limestone may initiate places of weathering disintegration. These material anomalies were less important

FIG. 5—*Moisture staining from water absorption or vapor condensation:* (a) *on a pedestrian bridge;* (b) *on an office facade.*

FIG. 6—*Effect of ettringite formation on some travertine stones:* (a) *mortar expansion causing buckling of cap stones;* (b) *mortar expansion causing splitting of anchor pocket.*

FIG. 7—*Moisture permeability in 3 in. (76.2 mm) or thicker cubic stock: (a) moisture discoloration on the exterior surface associated with water condensation on the interior stone face; (b) sedimentary rock can show substantial water permeability; metamorphosis rock experiences vapor transmission.*

in earlier thicker stone uses greater than 3-in. (76.2-mm) cubic stock. With stone 2 in. (50.8 mm) and under, planes of weathering weakness can pass through the entire thickness, resulting in potential freeze-thaw damage that can cleave the stone piece into separate parts. Figures 1a and 1b show examples of possible typical weathering sites that could lead to material separation.

Bowing of thin marble can occur as shown in Fig. 2a. This is believed caused by a permanent hysteresis growth in the stone due to a differential temperature or moisture change through its thickness. Generally convexed outward, the phenomenon can be concaved inward depending on boundary and gradient conditions. Figure 2b shows the curling of precast concrete panels faced with thin veneer stone. Shrinkage of the concrete back-up slab generally results in outward convexed curvature.

FIG. 8—*Effect of failure to accommodate differential building movements:* (A) *from restrained vertical movement;* (B) *from accumulated horizontal movement.*

FIG. 9—*Investigation of torsional twist at a spandrel beam:* (a) *exterior view showing spandrel panel configuration;* (b) *view of testing the out-rigger torsional-resisting framework.*

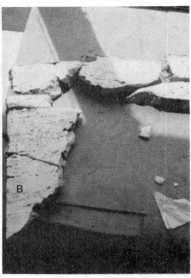

FIG. 10—*Effect of high wind forces at wall corners and roof eaves:* (A) *failure at a top coping corner;* (B) *fragments from failure.*

As stone usage becomes thinner, the degree of vitrification between grain boundaries, as in igneous rock like granite, may become a limiting strength feature. In ceramic engineering, ideally the grain size should be less than one-tenth the material thickness to minimize the limiting effects of grain boundary vitrification. Large grains relative to veneer thickness should be avoided in igneous stones. Figures 3a and 3b are views of relatively large grains.

To enhance their color hue, granite surfaces have been flame treated in recent years (Fig. 4a). The user of this technique must realize that such heat treatment of the surface causes microcracking of the stone thickness, reducing the expected flexural strength. When used, testing for the modulus of rupture of the treated stone should be undertaken (Fig. 4b).

Stone as it lies in the ground may be saturated with groundwater containing organic or inorganic materials. When exposed on the surface, such "quarry sap" may cause a temporary wet, blotchy appearance, as shown in Figs. 5a and 5b. With time, such appearance will generally disappear, water by evaporation and some organic staining by oxidation. Sometimes the mottled appearance will return after prolonged rain periods because of atmospheric pollutants in industrial atmospheres.

As spotting mortars are widely used in stone veneer systems, occasionally the setting time of such spots is reduced by mixing gypsum with portland cement. Under ideal wetting-drying and/or heating-cooling cycles, such material systems can form the mineral ettringite with time. Ettringite formation can result in high expansive forces that can displace stones, crack kerfs, and damage anchorage. Figures 6a and 6b show some views of the effects of ettringite formation on travertine panels.

The thinner the stone, the shorter the time required for water to permeate its thickness. When stone was 3-in. (76.2-mm) cubic stock or thicker, water permeability was of little concern. However, as evident in Figs. 7a and 7b, moisture permeability may become important. The effect on staining interior finishes or the bond of water-sensitive adhesives at the inside surface may become important.

FIG. 11—*Unaccommodated differential movement between anchors produced horizontal stone cracking due to relatively rigid anchors despite the presence of a plastic slip sheet behind the stone:* (a) *overview;* (b) *close up.*

These are seven examples of material problems typically encountered by the authors. None is especially unique. The purpose is to make the reader aware of some possible material problems with stone veneers.

Design Problems

A frequently encountered design problem is inadequate differential movement accommodation. A brittle facade skin of thin stone veneer experiences movement, vertically and horizontally, relative to the supporting building frame to which it is anchored, due to temperature and moisture changes in the stone itself as well as in the frame. Inadequate

FIG. 12—*Effect of an inadequate internal drainage and weep systems:* (A) *inadequate weephole drainage leads to horizontal heaving of panel from ice formation;* (B) *break of vertical joint caulking and flashing causing uncontrolled water to flow to the interior.*

horizontal and vertical movement joints can produce the kind of distress noted in Figs. 8A and 8B.

Typical spandrel-window treatment is shown in Fig. 9a, showing a horizontal soffit, vertical fascia, and sloping sill configuration. Such configurations can produce a torsional twist on the frame spandrel beam supporting the floor. When glass windows are framed into the window opening, the maximum torsional deflections must be restricted to under 1/4 in. (6.35 mm) to avoid glass breakage. The case shown experienced sufficient angular twist to prevent the window installation without special spandrel torsional reinforcing.

Facades of high-rise buildings experience high wind forces at the wall corners and roof eaves. A failure of this kind is shown in Fig. 10A. Shedding vortices of severe intensity are experienced at such locations, requiring both special stone loading and detailed anchorage behavior analysis. Rule-of-thumb stone thickness and anchorage sizes cannot be relied upon. Full-scale structural mockup tests are frequently justified.

The thin, deep wall planes of stone veneer spanning horizontally and resting for vertical support on relatively shallow frame spandrel beams may be forced to participate as thin, deep beams before the frame spandrel assumes its full load. The same idea is true of relatively large vertical areas of opaque, thin stone walls that experience side-sway effects due to relative rigidities before a more flexible wind frame can fully participate. This is especially true at building corners and flat roof edges where wind suctions are particularly high in magnitude. Figures 11a and 11b illustrate these ideas.

As all thin veneer stone systems have joints between stones, these are subject to water leakage. Further, where stone veneers meet window and door curtain wall systems, joints

FIG. 13—*Effect of:* (a) *improper dowel liner orientation; or* (b) *corroding spline reinforcement.*

are created. Such joints will give rise to water penetration requiring an adequate internal drainage and weep system. Figures 12A and 12B show some effect of an inadequate system resulting in internal water staining of the architectural finishes, freeze-thaw rupture of flashings, or lateral displacements due to heaving action of water accumulations.

Seemingly simple design features such as the orientation of the dowels in gravity liner supports or the use of noncorrosive resistance spline reinforcement can result in failed panel systems as shown in Figs. 13a and 13b.

Figures 14a and 14b illustrate the necessity to consider the effect of cyclic fatigue loading on the stone veneer system. During a minimum 50-year life of a building facade, repeated wind loading inward and outward occur. The interaction between the metal anchorage and the stone veneer may require design consideration of the material endurance limits.

FIG. 14—*Simulated effect of fatigue cyclic loading on flexible facade anchor systems:* (a) *view of testing apparatus;* (b) *a failed specimen.*

Anchorage Problems

The inadequacy of a "blind" anchorage technique or the lack of a positive means of mechanical anchorage is shown in Figs. 15a and 15b. The attempt to push simultaneously seven anchors "blind" into the mortar pockets defeats reasonable expectations. Once in place, there is no way to check the security of the anchor penetration into the mortar pockets. This methodology fails to meet the expectation of a positive means of mechanical anchorage.

As stone materials are brittle in nature, they are very sensitive to stress concentration in kerfs or other reentrant corners. Unfortunately, failures of the backside of such anchorage arrangements can occur undetected. A typical stress concentration failure is shown in Fig. 16a. The magnitude of the stress-concentration strain is very dependent on the care with which the grove is cut. Rounded internal corners have lower stress concentrations than sharp right angle ones. Care in grinding such groves is critical.

An extension of the idea shown in Fig. 16b is the use of a semicircular cut to receive a round metal disc anchor. Aside from the stress concentration effect already noted, such pocket-like cuts can fill with water or expansive mortar components (like gypsum and portland cement discussed earlier). The former can cause expansion failure from freezing and the latter from ettringite formation pressures. Again, the bursting of such pockets can be hidden from view if the backside fails. Figures 17a and 17b represent a typical front face failure, probably due to freezing water.

Unaccommodated differential movement can occur between anchors, particularly if the anchor passes through a hole in the stone without the benefit of a stress-concentration-reducing grommet. Figures 18a and 18b are an example of such a condition.

When anchorages to the same piece differ as to material and shape (for example, copper wires versus stainless steel strap) as shown in Figs. 19a and 19b, the probabilities that all anchors will engage simultaneously when subjected to lateral load is very unlikely. The

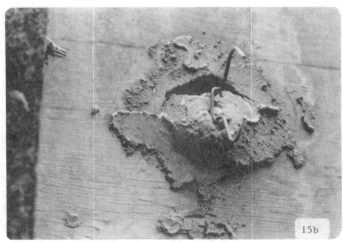

FIG. 15—*Example of "blind" anchorage techniques: (a) "blind" spring clip mounted in the panel back; (b) typical mortar pocket to receive the spring clip.*

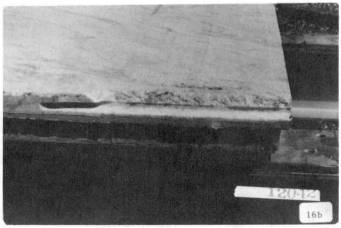

FIG. 16—*Brittle stress concentration failures at kerfs or reentrant corners:* (a) *a typical kerf profile at a shelf angle bent plate;* (b) *a typical kerf shear failure due to lateral wind load.*

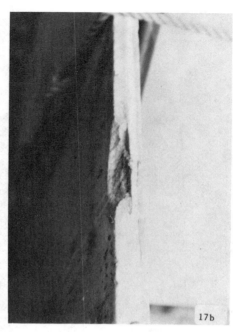

FIG. 17—*Segmental anchor pocket cut by a circular saw:* (a) *view with an inserted strap anchor causing rear failure;* (b) *view of failed pocket after panel removal.*

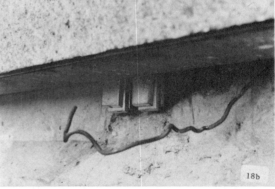

FIG. 18—*Proper position of shelf angle can be hampered by wide variation in air space distance causing:* (a) *excessive outward panel placement on the horizontal leg;* (b) *excessive thickness of shim spacers.*

FIG. 19—*Illustration of dissimilar anchorage materials in the same stone piece:* (a) *twisted copper wire anchor;* (b) *stainless steel strap anchor.*

FIG. 20—*Excessive bending of anchor strap under lateral loading:* (a) *note outward panel displacement;* (b) *close up of a bent strap anchor.*

FIG. 21—*Strap anchor in caulked joint causes edge splitting failure because anchor pocket not cut deep enough.*

hazard of progressive failure from the most highly stressed anchor to the less-stressed anchors can happen. A mixture of twisted wire and flat strap anchors is particularly vulnerable as shown in Fig. 19a.

The ability of an anchor to engage its resistance as soon as the lateral load is applied is crucial to thin stone veneer structural success. The distance from the strap bend line to the screw anchor greatly controls the engaging resistance (Figs. 20a and 20b). If not all anchors are engaged simultaneously, warping of the stone surface will tend to occur, producing critical flexural stresses.

FIG. 22—*Failure to remove a temporary shim or spacer.*

FIG. 23—*Omission of stainless steel dowels from a panel liner.*

Workmanship Problems

Soft-caulked joints around stone pieces, under horizontal shelf angles, or vertically in expansion joints are defeated in their intended differential movement accommodation if they have pieces of hardened spotting mortar in them. Figure 21 shows the localized splitting failure that may occur in the stone unit with the existence of such hard inclusions.

Similar effects can occur due to failure to remove temporary shims or spacers (Fig. 22). Such careless procedures can result in stacking effect over several stories until the accumulated stone dead-weight exceeds anchor capacity, and the collapse of many stones may be experienced.

Figure 23 illustrates the effect of clogged drains and weephole systems from careless caulking or mortar droppings. Besides perhaps causing internal leakage, outward heaving

FIG. 24—*Missing panel anchor tie at panel slotted hole.*

FIG. 25—*Inadequate grouting of panel anchor ties into a concrete block cell.*

of stone units and cracked kerfs can occur. The difference in the effect of a poorly designed or a poorly installed drainage system is difficult to show in terms of resultant failure. Necessarily, the categories discussed in this paper overlap.

Careless cutting of edge kerfs can result in premature failures due to excessive stress concentration or excessive thin edge pocket diaphragms. Where kerfs are factory cut, this is seldom a problem; only when hand tool techniques are used on the job site is this usually a problem (Fig. 24).

FIG. 26—*Omission of a panel boundary soft joint.*

The negative consequences of missing or unattached anchors is obvious. Collapse of whole stone units or pieces thereof can happen, endangering passersby. Besides missing or unattached anchors (Fig. 25), various substitutes for a positive means of mechanical anchorage can be devised by site workmen that can vary from "chewing gum to bailing wire" (Fig. 26).

Conclusion

The reader has been exposed to a variety of field problems encountered by the authors in investigating thin stone veneer. Inherently there is overlap in the categories. No attempt has been made to arrange the sequence discussed in order of frequency or severity. The problems discussed are presented as typical. The user of thin veneer stone systems is well advised to consider the reality that such problems have existed and may wish to devise steps in his own application to prevent them from arising.

Bibliography

Amrhein, J. E., and Merrigan, M. W., "Marble and Stone Slab Veneer," Masonry Institute of America, 1986.
Handbook of Indiana Limestone, 1982–1983.
Kaiser, E., "A Fundamental Factor in the Weathering of Rocks and Comparison of the Chemical Weathering of Stone in Buildings and Nature," *Chemic Der Erde,* Vol. 4, No. 2, 290–342 B.S.A., 1929 No. 1561.
Kessler, D. W. "Physical and Chemical Tests on the Commercial Marble of the United States," Technical Paper No. 123, U.S. Bureau of Standards, Washington, DC, 1919.
Kessler, D. W. "A Study of Problems Relating to Maintenance of Interior Marble," Technical Paper 350, U.S. Bureau of Standards, Washington, DC.
"Marble Design Manual," Marble Institute of America, Farmington, MI, 1983.
"Marble Engineering Handbook," AIA File No. 8B1, Marble Institute of America, Farmington, MI, 1960.
Schaffler, R. J., "The Weathering of Natural Building Stone," Department of Scientific and Industrial Research (British)," Building Research Special Report No. 18, 1932.
"Specificiations for Architectural Granite," National Building Granite Quarries Association, Inc., West Chelmsford, MA, 1972.
Stradling, R., "Effects of Moisture Change on Building Materials," Research Bulletin No. 3, London, 1928.
Winkler, E. M., "Stone: Properties, Durability in Man's Environment," Springer-Verlag, 1973.

Alex S. Gere[1]

Design Considerations for Using Stone Veneer on High-Rise Buildings

REFERENCE: Gere, A. S., "**Design Considerations for Using Stone Veneer on High-Rise Buildings,**" *New Stone Technology, Design, and Construction for Exterior Wall Systems, ASTM STP 996*, B. Donaldson, Ed., American Society for Testing and Materials, Philadelphia, 1988, pp. 32–46.

ABSTRACT: Due to substantial advancement of quarrying and fabrication methods, natural building stone has become available in thinner slabs in a wide variety of finishes, shapes, and sizes and has also become relatively less expensive than some of the other building cladding materials, which producers were forced to keep raising prices for due to the energy crisis of the 1970s.

This relatively low fabrication cost, together with the development of the various suspension systems and the advancement of the fabrication technology of anchoring components, makes the durable and relatively maintenance-free natural building stone more desirable to use to clad the increasing number of high-rise buildings built worldwide.

But, together with increased use of building stone, the number of expensive failures are also increasing. Sometimes facade failures can endanger public safety, and the cost to repair or reconstruct distressed stone facade can exceed its original cost.

The author, during the last 30 years, has investigated numerous miscellaneous types of failures of building stones of sedimentary, metamorphic, and igneous origin on building facades, as well as on exterior plaza installations.

KEY WORDS: stone veneer, exterior wall systems, stone technology

The most widely used natural stones for cladding high-rise buildings are:

1. *Limestone.* Layered rock of sedimentary origin, usually produced by precipitation of calcium carbonate ($CaCO_3$) and/or magnesium carbonate ($MgCO_3$) from ocean water with a minor-to-major admixture of skeletal organisms of various types. Strength and durability of the rock depends primarily on the degree of cementation. Because of the relative solubility in acid of the constituent minerals (calcite and dolomite), limestone is relatively subject to attack by acid rain and other acid pollutants in the atmosphere.

2. *Marble.* Limestone recrystallized (metamorphosed) under heat and pressure, giving rise to a relatively coarse-textured rock with tightly interlocked grains of calcite and/or dolomite. The porosity/permeability of marble is typically very low, but its susceptibility to destructive attack by acid is comparable to that of limestone.

3. *Granite.* Granite and related rocks are igneous, crystallized at depth from molten silicate rock material (magma). Granite and related rocks have a variety of colors and textures [see Annual Book of ASTM Standards, Vol. 04.08, ASTM Standard Definitions of Terms Relating to Natural Building Stones (C 119-86)].

[1] Vice president, Stone Tech, Inc., New York, NY 11101.

From the point of view of installation methods, limestone, marble, and granite claddings can be categorized as follows:

1. *Job set* installations, such as:
   a. Stone veneer conventionally installed and anchored piece by piece to a backup structure, usually from scaffolds or sometimes from the floorslab (Fig. 1).
   b. Mechanically installed stone veneer (without the use of cement mortar), anchored piece by piece to a metal grid system, which in turn is secured to the building structure. Such installations are done either from scaffolds or from the floor slab (Fig. 2).
   c. Floor-to-floor panel installation, using thicker stone slabs extending from floor slab to floor slab usually without the use of scaffolds (Fig. 3).
   d. Stone veneer installed to curtain wall components, either similar to the glazing method or with the introduction of special aluminum extrusions for gravity and lateral supports. This is also done usually from the floor slab (Fig. 4).
2. *Preassembled* systems, having built larger panels in a shop under controlled conditions:
   a. To precast backing (Fig. 5).

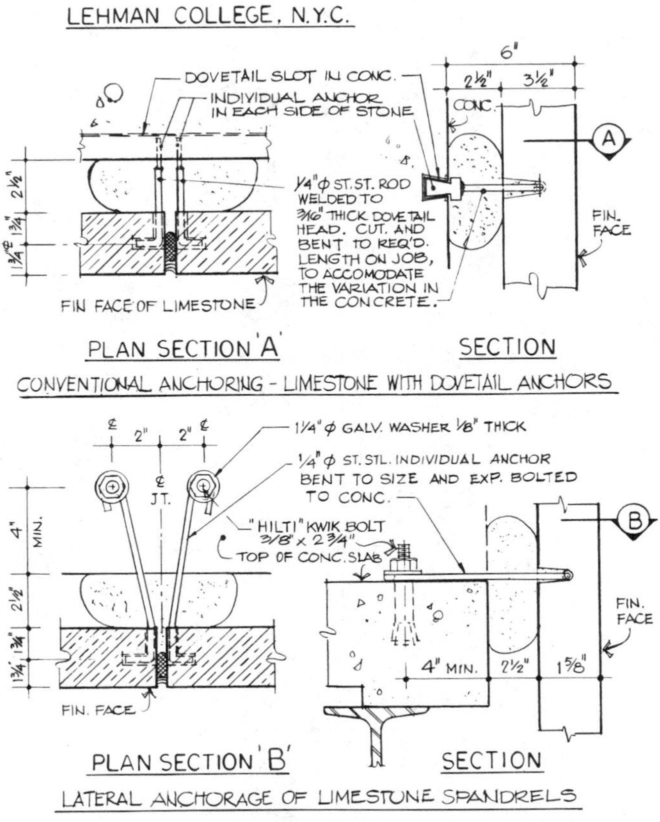

LEHMAN COLLEGE, N.Y.C.

PLAN SECTION 'A'   SECTION

CONVENTIONAL ANCHORING - LIMESTONE WITH DOVETAIL ANCHORS

PLAN SECTION 'B'   SECTION

LATERAL ANCHORAGE OF LIMESTONE SPANDRELS

FIG. 1—*Conventional stone installation method.*

REPUBLIC BANK - HOUSTON, TEXAS.

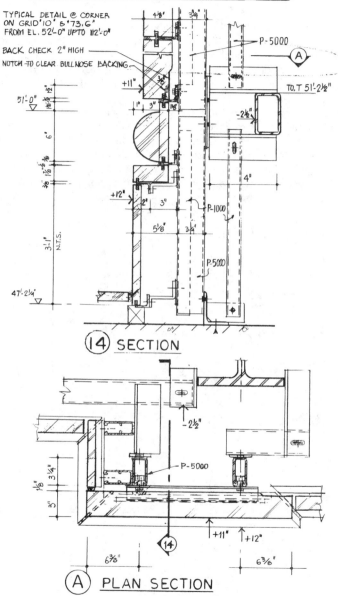

FIG. 2—*Mechanical installation method.*

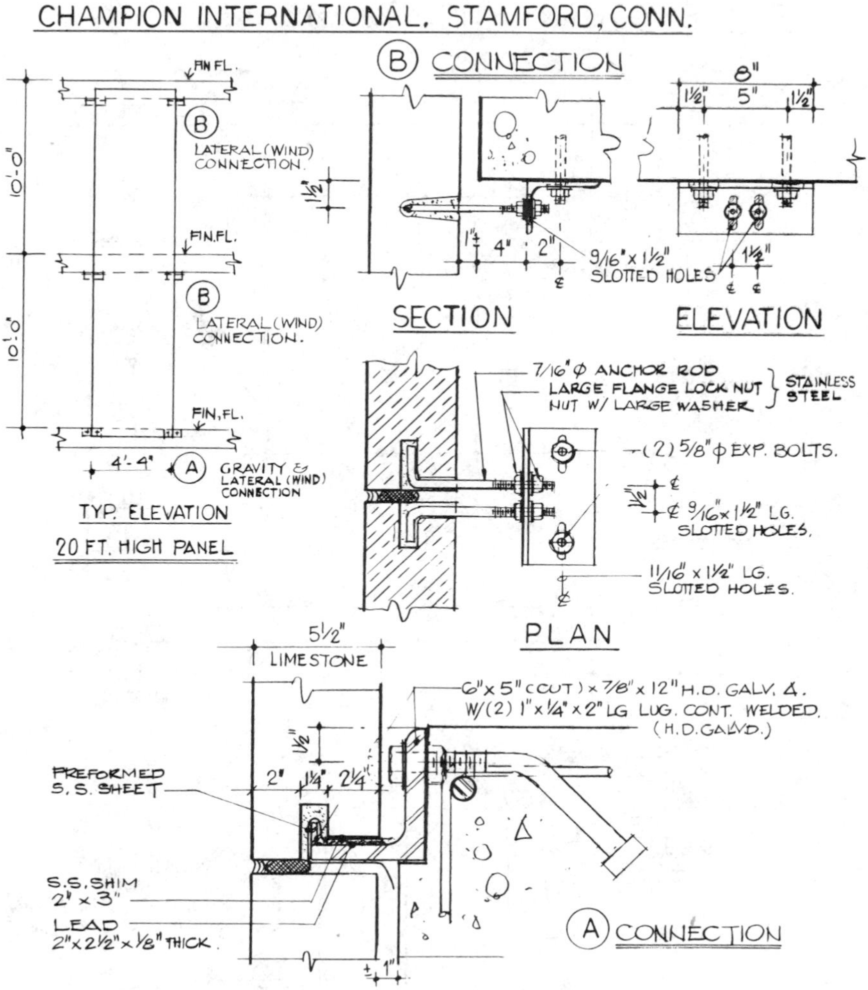

CHAMPION INTERNATIONAL, STAMFORD, CONN.

B) CONNECTION

FIN FL.

B
LATERAL (WIND)
CONNECTION.

FIN.FL.

B
LATERAL (WIND)
CONNECTION.

FIN. FL.

4'-4" A) GRAVITY &
LATERAL (WIND)
CONNECTION

TYP. ELEVATION

20 FT. HIGH PANEL

8"
1½" 5" 1½"

1"
4" 2"
9/16" x 1½"
SLOTTED HOLES
1½"

SECTION

ELEVATION

7/16" ∅ ANCHOR ROD
LARGE FLANGE LOCK NUT } STAINLESS
NUT W/ LARGE WASHER } STEEL

(2) 5/8" ∅ EXP. BOLTS.

℄ 9/16" x 1½" LG.
SLOTTED HOLES.

11/16" x 1½" LG.
SLOTTED HOLES.

PLAN

5½"
LIMESTONE

PREFORMED
S. S. SHEET

2" 1¼" 2¼"

6" x 5" (CUT) x 7/8" x 12" H.D. GALV. △.
W/(2) 1" x ¼" x 2" LG LUG. CONT. WELDED.
(H.D. GALVD.)

S.S. SHIM
2" x 3"

LEAD
2" x 2½" x ⅛" THICK.

A) CONNECTION

FIG. 3—*Floor-to-floor panel installation.*

b. To metal trusses or frames (Fig. 6).
c. To shop-assembled curtain wall units having stone, glass, and aluminum components prebuilt.

The approximate weight of stone veneer systems using 3-cm-thick granite or marble for *job set* installations (Section 1a) is approximately 17 lb/ft^2 (83 kg/m^2) or, when using 3-in. (7.62 cm)-thick limestone, approximately 37 lb/ft^2 (180 kg/m^2).

For mechanically installed systems (Section 1b) we have to add the weight of metal grids to the weight of the stone. The additional weight can vary from approximately 3 to 6 lb/ft^2 (14 to 29 kg/m^2).

Using 3-cm-thick granite or marble veneer on 6-in.-thick precast panels (Section 2a), we have to add approximately 75 lb/ft^2 (366 kg/m^2) to the weight of the stone veneer.

REPUBLIC BANK - HOUSTON, TEXAS.

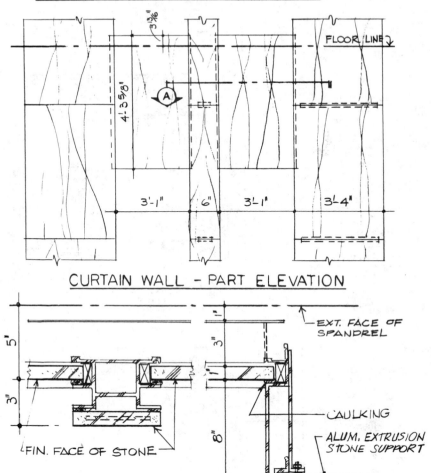

CURTAIN WALL - PART ELEVATION

PLAN SECT. A

FIG. 4—*Stone veneer, field applied to curtain wall.*

Using 3-cm-thick granite or marble veneer on steel trusses or frames (Section 2b), we should add the weight of the steel, which can vary approximately from 4 to 8 lb/ft² (20 to 39 kg/m²) depending on the span and the configuration of the truss design.

Design Principles

The functional requirements for the structure are established by the engineer of record, indicating the expectable movement and shortening characteristics of the structure and the maximum differential movement anticipated between the structure and its cladding.

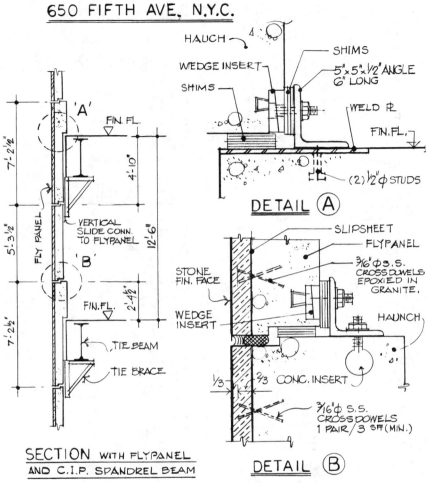

FIG. 5—*Stone veneer, preassembled on precast.*

The specifications, which can be written as design specifications or performance specifications, will establish the design criteria and part of the design considerations, such as windload, safety factors, possible seismic loading requirements, standard ASTM or special *mock-up* testing requirements, etc. Additional design information will be established on the architectural drawings and on the shop drawings, such as type, finish and thickness of the stone veneer, type size, and location of lateral and gravity supports, etc.

Selection of Stone

Aesthetic and economic considerations are strong factors in selecting the type and finish of natural building stone. The physical properties of most building stone used for cladding high-rise buildings are usually available from the fabricators in the form of standard ASTM test results previously done by independent testing laboratories. Such preliminary infor-

1333 H STREET WASHINGTON D.C.

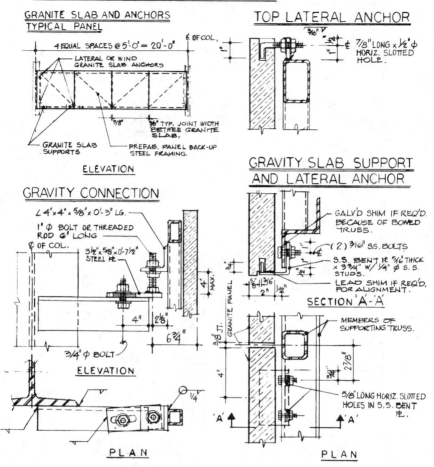

FIG. 6—*Stone veneer, preassembled on steel truss.*

mation can be compared with the minimal requirements for stone established by applicable ASTM standards:

1. For limestone, ASTM Specification for Limestone Building Stone [C 568-79 (1985)].
2. For marble, ASTM Specification for Marble Building Stone (Exterior) (C 503-85).
3. For granite, ASTM Specification for Granite Building Stone (C 615-85).

Knowing the environment, this comparison will help in the selection of the proper building stone and its proper finish.

Resistance to weathering and prevention of decay are also very important considerations when selecting building stone and its finish for cladding buildings.

Due to pollutants in the atmosphere, such as sulfates and carbon dioxide that form sulfuric acid and carbonic acid, rainwater may become very corrosive to stone. Therefore, when selecting building stone and its finish for exterior cladding, the resistance to atmospheric pollutants should be carefully considered.

Generally, the silicates in granite weather at a much slower rate than the carbonates in the limestone and marble. Acid waters and fumes can leach carbonate minerals in limestone and marble relatively quickly (10 to 50 years), whereas the same corrosive materials could alter feldspar minerals in granite very slowly (25 to 100 years).

Polished finish will reduce the surface porosity of natural building stone and increase its durability (resistance to weather); however, most calcite and dolomite marbles will lose their polished finish after prolonged exposure to atmospheric pollutants and to acid rain. Granite used for exterior cladding resists the atmospheric and climatic conditions very well especially when its exposed surface is honed or polished.

Humidity, freeze/thaw cycling, and large changes in surface temperature are also important considerations when selecting natural building stone, its finish, and its method of anchoring.

Domestic Indiana and Alabama limestones are widely used for exterior facing of municipal, commercial, and office buildings in the United States and have historically demonstrated good resistance to weathering. However, generally 3 in. (7.62 cm) or more thickness is used for facing such buildings with domestic limestone.

Lately, thin marble has often been used for exterior cladding utilizing 1-in. (25-mm), 1 1/4-in. (32-mm), or 1 1/2-in. (38-mm) thick slabs.

Some of the fine-grained *thin* (1 to 1 1/2-in. or 2.54 to 3.81 cm) crystalline marble slabs, due to thermal expansion and moisture, will release their stress of geological origin and, when cooling off, will not fully return to their original position. Thick marble slabs will resist such volume changes of the minerals on the surface, but thin marble slabs used for cladding can bow unless their anchoring method is designed to resist.

Flamed finish of a granite veneer will reduce its flexural strength. During the flaming process of the smooth granite surface, the quartz crystals expand more rapidly than the other surrounding minerals and are popping off, creating an uneven surface, which will better reflect the true color of the minerals than a sawn or low-honed surface finish would. The size of the hills and valleys of the flamed rock surface depends greatly on the sizes of the mineral grains of the granite.

Flame treatment causes microfractures on the surface, which will allow moisture penetration. The loss of the full stone thickness combined with the microfractures will not only reduce the flexural strength of the granite veneer but will also influence its durability by reducing its resistance to atmospheric attacks and to freeze-and-thaw cycles. The loss in flexural strength after flaming can vary from 5 to 35% depending mainly on the average size and physical properties of the rock-forming minerals, on the coherence of the rock, and on the presence of micro- or macrofractures in the rock. Consequently, when a flamed finish is desired, then increase of slab thickness should be considered.

Modulus of rupture and flexural strength tests modified by freeze-and-thaw cycles and testing the specimens so that the flamed surface is in tension will give an indication of the loss in flexural strength.

There is no ASTM standard to test the durability (resistance to weather) of a natural building stone. Lately, on a few large stone jobs, ASTM Test Method for Resistance of Concrete to Rapid Freezing and Thawing (C 666-84) has been specified for analyzing the resistance to freeze/thaw cycles of the stone. As ASTM C 666 does not represent the actual atmospheric and thermal conditions, a special durability test may be desirable.

An extensive testing program is necessary before ASTM standards can address the durability issue of natural building stone. Research data are needed for the loss in strength of sedimental, metamorphic, and igneous origin stones using different types of surface-applied finishes, when thin stone is used for exterior construction and when it is:

1. Exposed to freeze/thaw cycles.
   a. Vertically applied.
   b. Horizontally applied.
2. Not exposed to freeze/thaw cycles.
   a. Vertically applied.
   b. Horizontally applied.

The dry-to-wet ratio of the modulus of rupture of a thin section of natural building stone could also give an approximate evaluation of the durability of the rock. Erhard Winkler in his paper "Durability Index For Stone" (1985), prepared for the International Conference on Deterioration and Conservation of Stone, gives the relationship of the general stone evaluation as a function of dry-to-wet strength ratio based on the modulus of rupture (Fig. 7).

For some high-rise structures, large quantities of stone cladding are required. When selecting building stone for such buildings, it is also necessary that an experienced and qualified person (such as a cladding consultant) inspect the quarry and the fabrication plant to review if the quarry is able to supply all the required block quantities in the requested color, sizes, and quality on time, as well as if the shop is able to produce the required sizes, finishes, shop labor, and precision in the required sequence on time to meet the construction schedule.

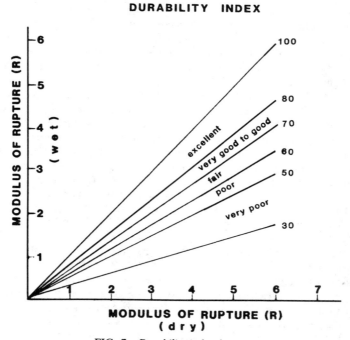

FIG. 7—*Durability index for stone.*

Testing Program

Modulus of rupture and water absorption by weight are the two most important physical properties for which ASTM has established minimum standards, such as ASTM Test Methods for Absorption and Bulk Specific Gravity of Natural Building Stone (C 97-63). The rate of water absorption is an important physical property when selecting building stone for exterior cladding because absorption and porosity have direct influence on moisture migration, weathering, strength, and, through these factors, on durability (weather resistance).

There are no minimum standards as yet for flexural strength of natural building stones. Testing the stone for compressive strength and for density could also be considered by the specifications. Five (5) specimens shall be tested for each test, preferably from different blocks. For modulus of rupture [ASTM Test Method for Absorption and Bulk Specific Gravity of Natural Building Stone (C 99-85)] and for flexural strength [ASTM Test Method for Flexural Strength of Natural Building Stone (C 880-85)], separate tests are required for wet and dry specimens in both directions: parallel to the rift and perpendicular to the rift. The direction of the rift must be indicated on the specimens by the manufacturer. The *average* of the test results should be used when calculating stone thickness for lateral anchoring.

For high-rise buildings where a large quantity of building stone veneer is used, it is common practice that a representative mock-up is built and tested in an independent testing laboratory. Water and air infiltration testing by static pressure is described by ASTM Test Method for Rate of Air Leakage Through Exterior Windows, Curtain Walls, and Doors (E 283-84) and ASTM Test Method for Water Penetration of Exterior Windows, Curtain Walls, and Doors by Uniform Static Air Pressure Differences (E 331-83) and structural performance testing by static pressure simulating positive and negative windloads as described by ASTM Test Method for Structural Performance of Exterior Windows, Curtain Walls, and Doors by Uniform Static Air Pressure Differences (E 330-84).

The design criteria for the maximum windloads for different areas of the high-rise buildings are usually based on a wind tunnel test study. The maximum allowable deflections relative to the structure are established by the performance specifications, and the true deflections of the wall components are measured on the full-scale testing mock-up with dial indicators and reported by the independent testing laboratory.

The thickness of the stone is controlled by the stress developed in the stone due to the load. (The stone itself is a rigid member and should not have any allowable deflection criteria.) Stone systems assembled on trusses, on struts, on grid systems, or assembled on curtain wall systems—depending on the size of the individual stone panels and on the method of anchoring—have maximum allowable deflection criteria established by the specifications between L over 240 to L over 360.

Once such a full-scale mock-up wall is built for testing, usually a dynamic pressure water infiltration test and a thermal cycling/condensation resistance test are also performed. Where it is deemed necessary, the performance specifications also call for seismic testing of the mock-up wall.

Simplified tests for water infiltration and for structural performance by static pressure are sometimes performed on the building wall using smaller test chambers built to the components of the wall on the jobsite.

Special anchor pullout or shear tests are designed if it's decided to test the desired methods of stone suspension and the factor of safety for the thickness of the stone veneer, as well as for the anchors (Fig. 8).

For a large job, it is prudent to test the quality of the stone in the shop by specially designed shop tests of a certain percentage of the slabs used for the project. Such shop

PEPUBLIC BANK OF NEW YORK

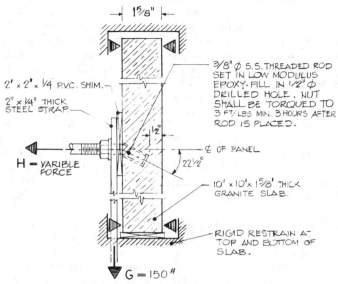

FIG. 8—*Special laboratory testing of stone anchor.*

testing is usually done by applying uniformly loaded weights on slabs or by using smaller test chambers for static pressure. The factor of safety for such shop tests is established by the specifications (Fig. 9).

Safety Factors

Natural stone will act in a manner consistent with the elastic theory of materials; however, we have to compensate for its characteristics of inconsistency in strength by using safety factors when calculating stone thickness for wind load or for anchoring.

When testing natural stones, test results in a close range indicate a stone with more consistent physical properties, while test results in a wider range show the weaker and stronger zones in that specimen.

A wide margin of safety is needed not only to meet the varying strength of the building stones but also to provide for handling, transportation, and erection abuse, for deterioration in strength of the stone after it is placed in the wall due to environmental attacks and normal expansion and contraction, freezing cycles, or other external forces.

Since the basic chemical and physical characteristics of natural building stone are determining factors of its strength and durability, it is recommended by the author that when calculating slab thickness for wind load, for handling, transportation, and erection, and for lateral anchoring that different safety factors be used for the sedimentary, metamorphic, and igneous rocks so that the safety factor will reflect not only the range of spread in the test results but will also agree with the general chemical and physical characteristics of the rock.

Using a minimum of five specimens from different slabs, it is recommended by the author that the spread of these test results compared to the *average of the test results* of the five specimens be converted to safety factors as described in Table 1.

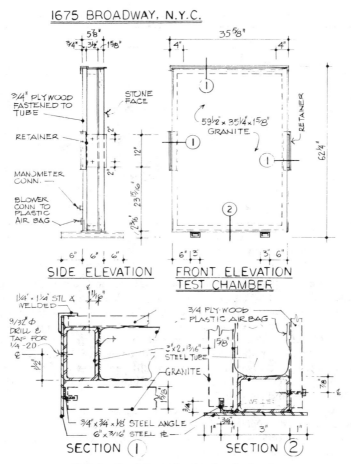

FIG. 9—*Special test chamber for shop testing.*

It is also recommended, when possible, that the full-scale anchoring system be laboratory tested in lieu of solely relying on calculations. Based on a minimum of five pull-out test results for anchoring stone, one can use the same safety factors which are recommended in Table 1 for calculating the stone thickness for wind load.

As a general rule, natural building stone possesses higher strength in a direction at a right angle to the bedding planes than in any other direction. All blocks should be slabbed in the same direction in relation to the bedding planes because the characteristics of the graining and veining are likely to change with the direction of the slabbing. Sandstones, due to their sedimental origin, should be slabbed parallel to the bedding plane.

Due to the tolerances and other "field conditions" allowed for in erecting steel structures or pouring concrete structures, the setting space behind a stone panel may have large dimensional variations. Other possible discrepancies such as missing or misplaced inserts, incorrect supporting components, etc. suggest that the design of all anchoring devices be for the worst condition and to follow American Institute of Steel (A.I.S.C.) specifications for allowable stresses.

TABLE 1—*Recommended safety factors for calculating stone thickness.*

Spread in Test Results (Compared to the Average of the Test Results)	Safety Factor for Windload	For Lateral Anchoring
IGNEOUS ROCK		
Up to 10%	3	4.5
10 to 20%	4	6.0
Over 20%	6	8.0
METAMORPHIC ROCK		
Up to 10%	4	6.0
10 to 20%	5	7.5
Over 20%	7	10.0
SEDIMENTARY ROCK		
Up to 10%	5	7.5
10 to 20%	6	9.0
Over 20%	8	12.0

Jointing

Qualified experienced persons should design, specify, and detail the joints, sealants, gutters, and methods of ventilation and drainage used for high-rise buildings clad with natural stone. Water is an enemy and might cause stains, induce galvanic action between dissimilar materials, create cracks while freezing and thawing, and possibly lead to structural failure. High-rise buildings deform, expand, and contract thermally or sway in the wind. Water constantly attacks the skin of the building, trying to enter into the cavity with the help of the porosity of materials, the wind, the pressure difference between the exterior and the cavity, the capillary action, and condensation. The expanding force of the freezing cycles can cause deterioration and structural damage.

An experienced, qualified person first gets acquainted with the structure, anticipated building movements, and expected tolerances and climatic conditions and is then able to establish the jointing conditions, joint sizes, and the type of sealant which will provide the best performance for the skin of the building.

Sealants need backup materials which compress easily and do not bond to the sealant. Most sealants require primers for better adhesion to natural stone. Particular care is necessary to have clean joints to insure proper adhesion.

Closed cell joint fillers are nonabsorbant to water. If the ambient temperature is very hot, or if punctured, or if overcompressed, the closed cell joint fillers might cause bubbling of the sealant while releasing gases. Open cell, sponge-type joint fillers have water absorption characteristics. Kerfs and holes in the tops of stone must be filled with compatible sealants.

In general, larger stone slabs have greater mechanical and thermal movement, and therefore more stress is put on small joints. However, reducing the stone panel sizes will increase the number of joints with more potential for human error, imperfections in installation, and more erosion of joint sealants due to constant attack by the elements.

Mistakes are made not only during the design stage but also during the application. It is advisable that an experienced inspector review the joint conditions and provide special sealing design for "job conditions."

No cladding is perfectly waterproof. Sooner or later water will find its way behind the stone cladding. Condensation also produces moisture. Therefore, water must be let out from the cavity behind the cladding. Properly designed and installed ventilation, weepholes (slots), gutters, and flashing serve this purpose.

Cladding Connections

The designer of the cladding system must be familiar with and understand the building structure and all other components of the cladding. After the engineer of record is consulted for the anticipated building movements, all possible combinations of the building and cladding movements shall be anticipated.

Transmission of loads from the building structure or from the backup supporting structure to the cladding through the connections must be accommodated without resisting them. This is done usually by sliding connections. If transmission of such loads is not prevented, it could lead to the development of such forces which will cause cladding failure.

The connections should be designed to be as simple as possible and as few types as reasonable, so that the possibility of using components at incorrect locations is reduced.

Stone panel suspension design is based on the design criterion established by the specifications and by applicable building codes.

The connections should be sufficiently adjustable to overcome tolerances in building construction and tolerances in stone fabrication. Connections should be located so that they will be accessible to the stone setters for adjustments during erection. Connection designers should recognize that it may become necessary to remove and replace any stone slab at a future date. With proper design, replacement can be done without any major alteration and expense.

When a poured-in-place reinforced concrete structure is clad with building stone, it is advisable that the cladding installation start only after the poured-in-place structure is completed and has cured adequately to accept additional loads.

Compressive strength is the strongest physical property of the building stone, therefore load-bearing connections should be located under the bottom joint, or, in case gravity supports must be concealed, as close as possible to the bottom joint.

Lateral anchors are usually placed in the joints between cladding panels. The number and the distribution of the lateral anchors should be determined by calculations and in conformance with the applicable building code. Such calculations are based on the forces to which the cladding will be subjected and calculated for all mechanical stresses to which they could be subjected: compression, tension, shear, bending, and torsion.

The use of round holes in stone to receive anchors or dowels is preferable to the use of slotted holes (kerfs), and individual anchors are preferable to "splittail" anchors or "drop dowels." Attention is required during the connection design to prevent stress concentrations at the anchor holes or kerfs. The use of nonstaining, fast-curing silicone or high-modulus polyurethane sealant in the anchor holes or kerfs is recommended.

TABLE 2—*Compatibility chart for metals often used for exterior stone installation.*

	1.	2.	3.	4.	5.	6.
1. Cast iron	Yes	Yes	Yes	No	No	No
2. Coated steel	Yes	Yes	Yes	Yes	Yes	Yes
3. Galvanized steel	Yes	Yes	Yes	X	Yes	No
4. Stainless steel 302 or 304	No	Yes	X	Yes	X	No
5. Aluminum 6061 or 6063	No	Yes	Yes	X	Yes	No
6. Brass or Bronze	No	Yes	No	No	No	Yes

X = compatible if not exposed within

2 miles of a body of salt water

All metals in direct contact with stone should resist corrosion and be nonstaining. Anchors not in direct contact with stone can be hot-dipped galvanized for exterior work. Above all, care shall be taken to avoid galvanic corrosion using noncompatible metals together without a proper isolator (Table 2).

For exterior gravity and lateral anchors embedded in holes or kerfs in with stone cladding, the use of 302 or 304-type stainless steel is recommended. Hot-dipped galvanized carbon steel gravity anchors have a heavy zinc coating which will prevent corrosion for many years. Drilled holes or rethreaded holes are a potential source of corrosion. Electrogalvanizing does not provide reliable protection for exterior anchoring. Electrogalvanized anchors are liable to scratch and rust.

Conclusion

The architect, the structural engineer, and the cladding consultant are the members of the design team which are responsible for the aesthetic requirements, the selection of the natural building stone and its finish, as well as for the preparation of the specifications and establishing the functional requirements for the building.

The design team must work closely together with the general contractor, the stone contractor, and the owner for the mutual goal, which is the timely completion of a functional cladding, free from future failures, in an economic manner.

The proper design, detailing, and specifying of a well-engineered building envelope of itself will not insure these mutual goals without controlled inspection by qualified persons. Only adequate inspection can prevent cladding failures due to unskilled or negligent erection operations or due to field conditions which deviate from the designed conditions.

Marc Heinlein[1]

Selection, Purchase, and Delivery of Building Stone—the Obstacle Course

REFERENCE: Heinlein, M., **"Selection, Purchase, and Delivery of Building Stone—the Obstacle Course,"** *New Stone Technology, Design, and Construction for Exterior Wall Systems, ASTM STP 996,* B. Donaldson, Ed., American Society for Testing and Materials, Philadelphia, 1988, pp. 47–53.

ABSTRACT: This paper discusses the relationship of the stone testing and evaluation procedures to the overall contract for stone curtain walls, construction scheduling, and quality control. Examples of three recent buildings in New York City will be used to illustrate the subject.

KEY WORDS: building stone, stone testing, stone curtain walls, quality control

Specification and Selection of Stone

Selection

Architects, designers, and owners invest large amounts of time, effort, and funds to choose the best material available at the correct budget cost. In recent years, this choice has been more and more often for stone, frequently granites. This is a good choice, but it is unusual when this choice is made in time and with the proper preparation. While stone is one of the oldest building materials used, it is surprising how little we know about it and its proper application.

Aesthetics—Color, grain, and finish are the first concerns to be satisfied. Usually, this begins in the sample rooms of the architects and stone suppliers. For space and handling, these samples tend to be small and not recent. Our first problems are beginning:

1. Small commercial samples are very indicative and may not represent the material correctly for color, grain, markings, range, occlusions, etc. I have witnessed embarrassing moments with persons who have spent a lifetime with stone and yet have been unable to identify materials correctly from small samples.
2. Many times the stone supplier labels the sample with a commercial rather than a generic name in order to protect his sources from potential competition. A number of these commercial names have been used for a sufficiently long time to become common usage and identify the material without difficulty. Instead, other names may be invented on the spur of the moment to provide an appearance of exclusivity or a relationship with an architecturally specified stone. In the latter case, a great deal of confusion can be caused (intended). Commercial names are all very well and the number and variety used for the same quality is a credit to the inventiveness of the industry, however, for the purposes of selection and

[1] Testwell Craig Laboratories, Lucca, Italy.

specification, a generic with the identification of the quarry should be noted. Also, it is useful to date the sample for approximate period of excavation. The architect and designer should always remember that there will be variations, some acceptable, some less so, and some not at all. I recommend that one remain very flexible.

Physical Characteristics—Once the architect has narrowed the number of stones that are candidates for the final selection, it is necessary to evaluate the physical characteristics of each stone and its application.

This includes the usual battery of tests for mechanical strength. Also important are determinations of the behavior of the stone in varying conditions of temperature and humidity since stone is in constant movement. The thinner the stone section and the larger the stone panel, the more this movement is apparent.

Tests for coefficient of absorption are usually performed on small samples. Absorption and porosity should be determined on typical panels with the specified finish and thickness.

Where possible, tests should be performed on blocks which have been excavated recently.

In order to avoid unpleasant surprises, the stone should be subjected to light and chemical conditions (including detergents) of the environment of its final destination. Both the color and the finish of the stone can be affected. There have been many cases where the stability of the color of a stone can vary from level to level and face to face within the same quarry.

Specification

As the properties and limitations of each stone become more clearly understood, it is important to ask repeatedly, because quarry and market conditions change, the following questions:

1. Will the stone be available in sufficient quantities to supply the project requirements on schedule?
2. What other projects are using the stone in consideration?
3. What other projects have used the stone and when, with what results?
4. Are the stone and applied finishes correct for field conditions and applications?
5. Is the stone adapted to the type of installation system specified?
6. Are block sizes sufficient for panel sizes?
7. What is the best thickness to use for the stone?
8. Within which range are the variations and occlusions which are inherent in the stone acceptable?
9. Can the desired visual effect be satisfied with the stone being considered?
10. Will the stone continue to provide this visual effect in time?

In other words, is the stone what we can accept within the numerous variables affecting the selection? Stone is a natural material but this should not be used against it as an excuse if a poor quality product is delivered. When used properly with intelligence and tolerance, I think most persons would agree that it is one of the most beautiful and suggestive building materials used.

As these various items are resolved, the architectural and engineering specifications should be amended and coordinated accordingly. It is very important that the specifications be clearly defined and without conflict since they are to become an integral part of the contract documents. There may be serious difficulties during production for establishing the acceptability or nonacceptability of stone in question when the specifications are remiss. Specifications for fabrication tolerances will have to be adapted to the stone and the capabilities of the selected manufacturer.

Stone Testing

The Need for Testing

The extensive testing of stone is becoming more and more recognized as a necessity. As additional information becomes available, the reasons for this become apparent; many commercial stones do not meet recommended minimum performance levels and structural characteristics are not within a normally accepted range of values. Minimum standards should be broken down by level and elevation of the structure and noted in the architectural specifications.

Numerous new systems for applying stone to building facing have been developed. Minimum test results previously recommended may no longer apply to many of these new methods of installation. Procedures for testing should be developed on a case-by-case basis as to how the stone is to be used.

Many of the test procedures and specimen sizes used today have little to do with the way the stone will be expected to work within the wall system developed for the project. Procedures and sizes established by ASTM are valid for comparison of characteristics between different stones and for establishing variations within each stone. Unfortunately, many of the specimen sizes suggested by ASTM are not large enough to permit the specimen to be a "representative" sample of the stone for an actual building.

Other issues regarding the difference between ASTM procedures and the practical application of the test results are specimen conditioning, thickness, and finish.

Test Procedures

Recently many engineers have used the specified ASTM procedures for the testing of stone during a preliminary phase. For precontract testing, the ASTM procedures are modified in order to permit larger specimen sizes, in particular for flexural testing, and to incorporate thicknesses and finishes specified for the project in question. It is not uncommon to find that some materials, which could not meet requirements for building codes in certain countries when tested according to the standard procedure of that country, were more than acceptable when tested under a modified procedure which reflected the use of the stone.

There should be a review of various ways different ASTM test procedures might be modified to reflect site conditions in a manner which would be acceptable for adoption as a standard. This should include testing for stone subject to thermal and chemical deterioration. The ASTM procedures create guidelines for the engineering community, are for points of reference, and do not represent absolute values.

The testing of stone for exterior use in facing and paving can be a lengthy process. For example, testing in various modes following freeze-thaw cycles can take several months. As a result, as much lead time as possible with a minimum of "fast-tracking" is highly recommended. Also, the list of tests can be extensive in order to cover the following:

1. Classification.
2. Chemical properties and composition.
3. Permeability and rate of absorption.
4. Specific weight.
5. Abrasion resistance.
6. Mechanical strength in compression, rupture, impact, and flexure.
7. Mechanical strength following exposure to freeze-thaw cycles or chemical conditions.
8. Thermal conduction.
9. Expansion, contraction, and warp in different conditions of temperature and humidity.
10. Resistance to prolonged and extreme conditions of temperature (fire) and humidity.

11. Resistance to insertion and extraction of mechanical fixings (anchors) used to attach the stone.

12. Compatibility with chemical fixings/bonds/fillers.

13. Color stability.

14. Other tests which may apply to special site conditions and interiors.

Examples

Testing is expensive and time consuming but is worth while whether or not problems develop. Following are some examples of results of late testing or the lack of testing:

Mold Growth—This could be for molds and fungi in a tropical climate: how to prevent it from occurring, and how to clean it when it occurs, using agents which will not harm the stone. An extreme case of this was viewed on an interior application of 3/8-in.-thick filled travertine panels in bathrooms in a luxury hotel in Indochina. Unfortunately, travertine cannot be expected to be 100% filled with normal procedures of parging and polishing. The fungus in question began to break out the parging and spread behind the travertine. Occasionally, the fungus would break out the travertine tile, and the odor and appearance were decidedly disagreeable. Many remedies were tried, none successful, and a good deal of damage and inconvenience was caused.

Cleaning—Improper cleaning methods for a honed white marble paving for the public atrium of an office building caused the following situation: rather than using clean water, water with dirt and detergents was used to wash the floor prior to the opening of the building. The detergent dissolved the dirt, which emulsified in the water and was rapidly absorbed by the marble. In order to prevent this from happening again, the floor was coated with a sealant (not tested) which proceeded to yellow. The remedy in this case was patterned carpeting. A case could be made for not having used this type of white marble but another.

Waxing—Another situation was not the fault of the stone, the manufacturer, the installer, or the maintenance crew, it was the fault of contaminated polishing wax for marble paving. Following cleaning and waxing of the floor, the stone proceeded to change color from pink to blue. This had happened on another project where the manufacturer had waxed red marble pavers which were red when crated and blue when unpacked, all caused by a fungus. The remedy was both inexpensive and successful in each case.

Acid Washed—On another project, a polished and flamed red granite on an exterior elevation had been soiled by cement slurry and fireproofing coming down from upper floors. The workmen who were instructed to do the cleaning decided that the fastest way would be to use an acid solution. We were never told which acids or solvents were used, but the mixture was sufficiently strong to burn the polish and turn the granite orange. It was necessary to replace the damaged panels.

Mechanical Tests—On another project, modified mechanical testing was done after approximately 15% of all exterior granite had been sawn into slabs, finished, selected, and approved for color. Each block sampled failed to meet the specifications. Also, a porosity problem was noted and all slabs cut to the original thickness were discarded because it was necessary to increase the thickness. This caused delays, difficulty with the supply and color match of the stone, and a series of problems for the fabrication and installation. The stone was set into a stick system and most of the metal components had been extruded as to the original thickness. As a result, it was necessary to adapt the new stone panel to the old anchoring system.

Radioactivity—Following the completion of exterior stone production for the headquarters of a large public mining company, a company chemist decided to run a chemical analysis on the granite used. He discovered a radioactive material (thorium) and issued a general memorandum which identified but did not specify the amount present. This memorandum caused panic throughout the organization. It was later determined that the amount was trivial and harmless. I was told that the design architect received a pair of lead underwear after the uproar died down.

These are only a few of the situations we have encountered which were due to lack of information concerning the material. There are many more and we have heard of many more again. The stone should be considered a factor which cannot be easily changed once it has been adopted. We have to work around it or substitute it if the changes which must be made to conform to the limitations of the stone are not feasible.

Production Testing

Once a stone has been selected and tested to the satisfaction of all properties, it is advisable to establish a testing program to be implemented during production. The types of testing normally requested are rupture and flexure, ASTM Test Method for Modules of Rupture of Natural Building Stone (C 99) and Test Method for Flexural Strength of Natural Building Stone (C 880), modified for project thickness, finish, and span between anchors. The frequency of testing can be determined in a series of ways.

Samples—Usually we recommend the sampling and testing of five blocks prior to beginning production. This testing often indicates the amount of deviation that can be expected in test results and the average performance of the stone. At this time the rate of testing can be decided: one series for one-block-in-five, one series per 5,000 ft^2 of slab destined for production, one series per 50 slabs, or other. When possible, sampling and testing should reflect all conditions of the slab during the precontract phase. Sampling and testing for contract stone and production stone should reflect the conditions of the slab that are acceptable.

Determination of Rift—The modes of testing are usually perpendicular and parallel to rift, wet and dry, with a minimum of three specimens per mode. The first problem is to determine the "rift" of the block. It is our experience that blocks can be excavated to maximum advantage from masses detached from the quarry wall. Often this means that the block is not necessarily running with the rift of the quarry bed. It is preferable to refer to the saw marks (lime marks) which are evident on at least one face of the specimen. Loading is made "perpendicular" or "parallel" to the saw marks left from slabbing. These sawmarks become the reference for the correct cutting of the granite panel; for example, results in the perpendicular mode are acceptable and parallel results are not. Rather than rejecting the block outright, the slabs from this block can be fabricated into panels with the saw marks running parallel to the span of the panel; loading would be perpendicular, the opposite for where parallel results were acceptable and perpendicular results were not.

Wet/Dry Testing—The preproduction testing of five blocks could also demonstrate whether the wet or dry condition is decisively stronger. This situation does occur with many stones. A case could be made for eliminating testing which is not "worst case."

In spite of all the precautions one can take in the selection of blocks and resulting slabs, there is almost always a percentage which will be under strength. This condition may not be imputable to the material or to the rift of the quarry. For example, improperly placed charges during exploration or excessive blasting during excavation can "unnerve" the crystalline structure of a granite in certain areas, and this disruption of structural integrity may not be apparent with a visual inspection only.

Quarry Assessment and Selecting a Manufacturer

Quarry Assessment

If at this point the owner, the general contractor, and the architect are still willing to face the building with a natural stone product, it is time to work closely with a group of suppliers and installers who are bidding for the stonework as well as the quarries from which the materials you are considering are available. Recently we have noted significant efforts by the stone industry to supply information and technical assistance. It is unfortunate that in the past this cooperation was limited or lacking. Most of the information available to architects and engineers in the past has been the result of field experience.

If the project requires a relatively substantial amount of the stone selected and must be excavated specifically for the project in question, it is advisable to make an independent study of:

1. Color and variations in grain and bedding of the quarry.
2. Excavation methods used past and present, eventual suspensions of operations and reason.
3. Rates of production and block sizes available, quarry conditions on a seasonal basis, development and clearing.
4. Quarry management and record, permits and licenses.
5. Block transportation from the quarry to factory site, estimated shipping times.

With answers to the items above, one should be able to determine the reliability and availability of the source of the material(s).

Selecting A Manufacturer

Regarding the selection of a manufacturer, much depends upon the scope of the work to be performed, the budget, and the schedule. In selecting a manufacturer, even through an importer or an installer, it is advisable to remember the following guidelines:

1. Evaluation of past and current performance on other projects and personnel.
2. Capacity and elasticity in production, possibility and availability of subcontracting facilities.
3. Equipment and level of investment and maintenance.
4. Sufficient financial strength to complete the order capitalization and bonding ability.
5. Access to selected stones, eventual experience and availability of inventories.
6. Experience with working drawings and construction schedules.
7. Availability of transportation and type of transportation for finished stone to the project site and shipping times.

Another factor in selecting the manufacturer can be the level of understanding between the supplier and designer as to the end result expected.

The architect must provide clear standards for the product ordered, and preliminary drawings should allow for as many eventual details and finishes as possible. The manufacturer and installer can only provide offers based upon the information they have received.

As the design status changes to reflect aesthetic or technical conditions, the different subcontractors should be advised immediately in case their costing should be affected.

The general contractor should inform itself as to the costs of any alternative materials and all unit prices affecting the fabrication of the stone.

All parties must coordinate design, engineering, and production schedules as to the availability and strength of the material. These conditions can change as demand for the material in question increases or decreases.

Information and pricing from the different suppliers should be confronted and questioned constantly for proper evaluation.

The owner and general contractor must place the order in time as to a realistic schedule.

While none of the above items or guidelines are new, it is discouraging how frequently they are not regarded, often to the detriment of the stone and the building. Since stone is a natural material, its use is affected by a series of factors which may not be known at the time of its selection. As a result, it is recommended that additional care and attention be provided early in planning for its use. When problems occur which cause serious difficulties, the stone is blamed and not the lack of planning. Stone is what it is. It will always vary in color, grain, strength, and availability. If you are aware of these conditions, if you can work with them, then the use of stone should prove to be a satisfying experience.

In closing, it is my personal opinion that stone should not be considered an industry. The working of stone will always remain a craft because of its very nature.

Design Criteria for the Use of Exterior Stone

Edward A. Benovengo, Jr.[1]

Design Criteria for Thin Stone/Truss Wall Systems

REFERENCE: Benovengo, E. A. Jr., **"Design Criteria for Thin Stone/Truss Wall Systems,"** *New Stone Technology, Design, and Construction for Exterior Wall Systems, ASTM STP 996,* B. Donaldson, Ed., American Society for Testing and Materials, Philadelphia, 1988, pp. 57–65.

ABSTRACT: The stone industry has experienced little change in construction practices over the last century, save the events of the last five years. The area of acute recent activity has been the advent of new, sophisticated stone-cutting systems. The offspring of this is the production of building stone of great face size with stone thicknesses of mere centimeters in lieu of inches. The thin stone panels can become an efficient stone envelope system when joined by dedicated support and other envelope components, thus creating a stone envelope assembly with obvious advantages over conventional stone construction.

The challenge for the design professional is two-fold in considering the use of thin stone wall systems. The initial challenge is one of aesthetics and design flexibility. The latter and more demanding challenge is the appropriate selection of materials, components, and assemblies to produce an integrated building envelope system which satisfies the particular criteria of the selected project. A primary need is the proper linking of expectations and capabilities.

The performance criteria established by the design professional will require a systematic review of materials, componentry, and performance criteria including stone properties, anchorage systems, material compatility, joint treatment, code limitations, and thermal, air, water, and moisture control systems. Additional concerns focus on limitations imposed by thin stone wall systems to the project design and construction.

KEY WORDS: thin stone truss wall systems, stone industry, stone-cutting systems, support panels

The stone industry has experienced little change in construction practices over the last century except for the events of the last five years [1]. One area of recent acute activity has been the advent of new, sophisticated stone-cutting systems from Italy. The offspring of this is the production of building stone of great face size with stone thicknesses of mere centimeters in lieu of inches. Whereas 4 to 6-in. (10.16 to 15.24-cm) stone depths were common industry standards, now 3-cm stone is common in the marketplace with even thinner stone in development. The thin-stone panels can become an efficient stone cladding system when joined by dedicated support and other envelope components, thus creating a stone envelope assembly with obvious advantages over conventional stone construction [2]. It should also be noted that such wall systems have the potential of more consistent assembly quality and faster on-site erection time if the systems are off-site, shop-fabricated panels. One very common form of thin-stone wall system is the use of stone prefabricated onto metal truss support panels. The stone/truss wall produces many particularly unusual considerations and is the topic of further discussion here.

---

[1] Architect, Skidmore, Owings & Merrill, New York, NY 10017.

The challenge for the design professional is twofold in considering the use of stone/truss wall systems. The initial challenge is one of aesthetics and design flexibility. The later and more demanding challenge is the appropriate selection of materials, components, and assemblies to produce an integrated building envelope system which satisfies the particular criteria of the given project for aesthetics, structural support, thermal isolation, air infiltration, water penetration, corrosion prevention, etc. A primary need is the proper linking of design expectations and construction capabilities.

The performance criteria established by the design professional will require a systematic review of materials, componentry, and performance criteria, including stone properties, anchorage systems, material compatibility, joint treatment, joint seals, code limitations, and thermal, air, water, and moisture control requirements. Additional concerns focus on limitations imposed by thin-stone wall systems to the project design and construction.

Most thin stone produced today is quarried and cut overseas. Since the Italian stone industry created the machinery for thin stone cutting, it was and still is common for rough block stone, quarried all over the world, to arrive in Italy for cutting to finished product. In recent years, with the purchase of these thin stone cutting machines, some quarries in the United States, Brazil, and elsewhere can enjoy a competitive position in the thin-stone cutting market. Cut stone shipping costs are primarily based upon weight first, then distance. On high-rise office buildings there is a significant potential for cost savings, due in large part to the reduced freight costs incurred to ship thin stone from the quarry, to the stone cutter, and then to the erector. This is especially true when, for example, a stone quarried in Africa is sent to Italy for cutting and polishing and then crated and shipped to the United States for final assembly. The distance a stone is shipped greatly contributes to freight costs. The use of a stone from the United States may not necessarily produce a significant cost savings due to shipping alone, but can provide the capability for these other quarries to provide their stone in reduced thicknesses and thus be competitive in the marketplace. Additional cost savings are factored into the thin-stone system since thinner stone materials will cost less and will require less anchors, supports, materials, and other appurtenances, all with the multiplying effect of cost savings. This series of events sparked much of the initial interest in thin stone use over the last five years.

Stone Selection

In reviewing thin stone for use on a given project, the first subject for review is the stone itself. An area of heated discussion is that of which stone types may be best suited for thin-stone application. Stone as a natural material is not of controllable quality and varies from species to species and within each species. A stone quality can even vary with location within the quarry. When visual selection criteria is added to the decision process, further limitations can develop. One of the major concerns of thin stone is the strength of the fabricated stone unit and the uniformity of strength through the cross section and face area. Stone is formed in nature by the bonding of various subcomponent elements in linear and nonlinear configurations. The bonding of these elements when cut gives the color and patterning much desired in the stone species. These bond patternings are commonly known as the gneiss of the stone. These same bonding characteristics can create either strengths or weaknesses in the stone which, when used in conventional (thick) construction, can be negligible considerations, but as the cut stone thickness decreases, these faults (which can penetrate through the entire thickness of the stone) become of great concern. Additional faults can be produced not naturally, but rather by the mechanical finishing of the stone. It has been noted in laboratory testing that the modulus of rupture for a stone specimen will vary with the finish [3]. Another cause of concern in thin stone is the microfracturing of stone when thermally finished. As with natural faults, mechanical faults are more critical with decreased stone thickness. Unless the stone from a given quarry is well known to the designer, it is mandatory to conduct a comprehensive stone testing program to establish the physical properties and limitations of the actual stone at its proposed thickness, face dimensions, and the anchorage system intended for use on the specific project.

Stone strength design is a topic of much industry discussion. On a given project the thickness of stone required will be dependent, in large part, upon the stone species, panel face size, stone finish, and the anchorage system, along with the established safety factor. The safety factor will ultimately determine the thickness of stone used for a given imposed loading and will directly impact the cost of the stone in ways previously discussed. With the decrease in stone thickness, we have also seen in the industry a decrease in the safety factor used for stone. This trend is a growing concern. As a matter of comparison with related building materials, the glass used in the windows of a thin stone exterior wall is traditionally designed with a statistical safety factor of eight lights per one thousand, or in equivalent mathematical terms, a safety factor of 2.5 [4,5]. This value, developed after extensive specimen testing, will create a condition by which under maximum design load the statistical probability of breakage for the glass is that of 8 units for every 1000 units used. Glass is perceived by the public as being fragile, breakable, and replaceable.

Stone, on the other hand, is perceived as being durable, impenetrable, and not in need of replacement during the life of the building. Stone and glass are similar in that both materials are brittle and can fail at areas of high stress or flaw. Failures are normally quick and dramatic. At present there are stone systems designed with factors of safety equal to or less than the factor of safety typically used for the glass in the adjacent windows.

At these lower factors of safety, stone failure at maximum design load is quite possible.

Another physical property to be evaluated is the weatherability of the stone. At SOM (Skidmore, Owings & Merrill), we have developed a technique to evaluate long-term performance to weather exposure based upon the acid rain microclimate of the specific project [6]. The testing has allowed our firm to reasonably anticipate the long-term weatherability of any stone and aid our clients in the selection of stone for their project. This process can be invaluable in the evaluation of several different species of stone from disassociated quarry sources.

On one project where two granites were in consideration for the high-rise facade, after testing, one stone exhibited greatly eroded surfaces with the creation of linear fissures and a demonstrated loss of gloss from the polished surface. These results, in addition to other considerations, led to the rejection of that stone. Curiously though, the stone our firm rejected was bought by another firm for a local project. This gave our firm a unique opportunity to field verify our testing. The stone in question, observed in place after a few years, has borne out our initial suspicions.

Performance Criteria

Once a given stone is selected, the process of creating a stone-veneered exterior wall system begins. Two initial considerations must be established, the first being the overall performance requirements for the entire assembly, the second being the specific requirements for componentry to achieve the overall assembly performance.

An exterior wall will be required to perform specific functions to be considered suitable for use on a building. Values of performance for such diverse functions as thermal barrier, moisture control and drainage, air infiltration, corrosion resistance, structural support, etc. must be set and determinations made as to how components alone and in combination are expected to perform. These values exist within the construction industry, but standards have not yet been established specifically for thin-stone wall assemblies by any construction industry group [7,8].

Anchorages and Supports

To simplify the analysis, it is best to start from the building exterior and visually walk through the wall assembly. The thin stone veneer is supported by anchors to transfer gravity and lateral loads to the panel support system. The type of anchors best suited for use is a variable, but several basics can be established. Though many materials are often proposed, the standard of the stone industry has been anchors of stainless steel, which have a long-proven track record. Based on current trends, the newer materials offered have no improvement, have no long-term success record, and therefore should be excluded. The reasons for this concern are as follows. A common and popular substitute for stainless steel anchors today is the use of anchors of aluminum. Aluminum anchors are less expensive and can be extruded to any profile to match the needs of any anchorage condition, no matter how unusual. Aluminum, though weaker and more ductile than stainless steel, can possess sufficient strength and stiffness to support stone at current reduced thicknesses and associated reduced weight. However, aluminum is not inherently corrosion resistant and is a relatively unnoble metal which reacts with other commonly used metals [9]. Further, some stones, such as limestone and marble, contain calcium carbonate, which is an alkaline material that can be liberated by water, the dissolved solution being an alkaline which can interact with the aluminum. The issue of anchor corrosion has never been a major topic since stainless steel (300 Series) is well known as a stable corrosion-resistant material with a long history of satisfactory performance. This topic will undoubtedly be a subject of much industry controversy as the use of aluminum anchors continues to grow. Depending on the style of anchor used, it is important to seal the voids in the stone/anchor pocket or kerf to prevent reservoir space for water migration and eventual freeze/thaw damage. It has become a common practice to fill this space with a caulking compound. It is important, however, to select a material which is nonbleeding, nonmigrating, and compatible with contiguous materials, including other sealants used in the stone facade. The stone/anchor pocket or kerf may also be filled with conventional stone setting materials, which are less complicated, especially when compared to the use of construction sealants, which as a product type are not developed for use as encapsulated bulk fillers.

Corrosion

The connection of the stone anchors to the support frame requires care as well. Since this internal framing zone will in all probability experience exposure to water, corrosion resistance is essential. Coatings are required for framing and other components of carbon steel. Traditional steel primers are insufficient to prevent corrosion of these primary components. Hot-dipped galvanizing will yield better performance. High-performance paint coatings also are available which are easier to use and less expensive than galvanizing. Both galvanizing and paint coating require the need of rigorous field touch-up in order to maintain the coating integrity during fabrication and erection, and both require rigorous shop and field inspection to verify compliance. High-performance coatings have an advantage over galvanizing in that these paint coatings can be designed to yield excellent dielectric separation of metal components and, in doing so, prevent galvanic corrosion, which is a very serious threat to building enclosures. Depending upon the method of attachment selected for securing the support framing to the building structure, competent field inspection of the connections and the corrosion barrier/coating installation is critical and should be a mandatory practice. It cannot be stressed too strongly that corrosion of any component premanently concealed and non-accessible in the finished work is an unacceptable practice.

Special attention should be given to the fasteners used to secure the stone anchors to the truss framing. Stainless steel anchors have long been a standard and are time proven. New systems have started the use of self-tapping/self-drilling steel screws. These new fasteners, from the metal siding industry, are produced in carbon steel alloys which do not afford equal corrosion resistance or strength. Further protective zinc or cadmium coatings offered on some fasteners can react unfavorably with contiguous stainless steel, galvanized steel, and aluminum components [9].

Another form of corrosion that stone/truss systems fall victim to is the area of dissimilar metals isolation. The metal components for anchors, fasteners, support frames, gutters, air barriers, etc. tend to be designed and fabricated from different types of metals. Proper isolation of these materials by the use of dielectric separators is mandatory to prevent galvanic corrosion. This task is not easily accomplished by all systems, but is an essential requirement. Again, the potential corrosion of any critical components, permanently concealed within the stone/truss wall, is unacceptable [9].

Truss Configuration

The configuration of the truss support framing is an important consideration with respect to integrating related wall components. The framing components can be a benefit or a hindrance to the integration of other stone/truss wall components which require a high degree of continuity and fidelity such as: the thermal barrier, air barrier, flashing, fire safing, vapor barrier, etc. The design and fabrication of the truss support framing must integrate the needs of the other components to be housed within the assembly. Failure to accomplish this integration is a shortcoming of many designs, because, typically, the components not essential to the stone attachment (that is, insulation, flashing, sealant, drainage) are not typically included by the stone erector in the stone panel unless specially demanded in the contract requirements.

The shape of the truss members must be such as to prevent the pooling of water on or within the support framing. For example, channel sections with upturned flanges or tubing shapes can trap and collect water. Tube sections may also be problematic with respect to corrosion protection since inner tubing surfaces are rarely treated, even to remove mill residues, and provide surfaces which can fall prey to corrosion.

The Thermal Envelope

The thermal envelope is a problematic area in present stone/truss wall systems. Stone trusses can be easily preinsulated (prior to installation) to provide a continuous opaque thermal envelope. Insulation located within the panel assembly is beneficial since the insulation can run continuously outboard of the building structure. The quality of the installation is also greatly improved when performed off-site in a controlled environment along with the stone/truss assembly. Insulating the truss zone is desirable from the perspective of performance characteristics, but problematic from the design and construction viewpoint since this zone will likely experience water penetration. Insulation materials which are not water-sensitive (foam plastics) may possess combustible ratings normally unsuitable to building code officials for use on project interiors. Further, during construction it is normal for window openings to remain vacant for some time interval before glazing begins. These wall openings allow rain to soak more preferable water-sensitive wall insulation and ruin the thermal barrier. Water-damaged insulation at column-face and spandrel-face locations may not be accessible for replacement. Temporary protection is mandatory. The proper use of fire safing must be coordinated with the truss configuration to allow the safing material to contact a continuous truss member. When the local building code requires the exterior opaque wall to be fire rated, the integrity of the stone/truss fire-rated thermal insulation is critical since these insulations are sensitive to damage from water. Similar to the thermal barrier, the exterior envelope air barrier/vapor barrier can suffer from the lack of continuity and from weather exposure. This is an area which needs careful attention.

Since the strength of stone is affected by whether the stone is wet or dry (wet stone typically has a modulus of rupture less than dry stone), it is recommended to leave an air space at the back face of the stone to allow water to run down to the drainage system and weep out. Water will penetrate the stone veneer at stone joints and through the stone itself. For these reasons it is not advisable to locate insulation on the backside of the stone since water will be held in contact with the stone for relatively long time periods with the potential to weaken the stone under load.

Joint Treatment

Joint design of stone truss walls adds a new challenge to building seal design. A hierarchy of joint sizes and types is created by the panelization of stone onto a truss. Stone mounted to a truss will provide in situ joints sized primarily for visual appearance, since movement will be negligible. Joints between trusses will be the primary movement joints for the exterior envelope. Joints at window interfaces may require additional installation tolerances for acceptance of work by that building trade. The allowable face width of a sealant joint in a stone/truss wall has definite limitations with direct relation to the stone thickness. Proper sealant joint design requires a compressed backer rod and sealant in the proper depth/width ratio. This ratio allows the elastomeric sealant to perform as a weatherseal during a full range of wall movement. As stone truss movement joints increase in face size, the depth (thickness) of stone available to retain the joint seal becomes a critical dimension. Again, 3-cm-thick stone appears to provide the minimum joint depth suitable for most movement joint requirements [10].

The building sealant and the anchor pocket or kerf sealant, previously discussed, must be compatible and guaranteed by the sealant manufacturer(s) for the intended use. The sealant must also be nonstaining and capable of full curing without the exudation of by-products which can stain the stone.

A common practice of many types of stone/truss walls utilizes only sealant as the building seal. Sealant by design is a product capable of performing over a broad range of dynamic conditions, but with a significant price—reduced longevity. Sealant in a stone/truss wall system is the shortest-lived material used in permanent construction and is, therefore, a poor choice for the only building seal. As a general practice, the use of a single building seal design or "single line of defense against air and water infiltration" in an exterior wall system will produce walls of much less success than similar walls with multiple lines of defense constructed into the assembly.

Drainage Systems

The single most problematic component of the stone/truss wall is to design an effective flashing system. Since the sealant joints between stone panels are commonly the only defense against water penetration into the stone truss assembly, it is essential to provide an effective flashing and drainage system. The traditional approach to flashing stone walls is to provide a system installed between the setting of adjoining stone panels within the normal construction sequence by a variety of building trades. The wall assembly is typically constructed with access from both inside and outside of the building simultaneously. Stone/truss wall systems are normally installed from the building interior only. Since no exterior access is commonly provided, it is impossible to design a stone/truss flashing system which requires installation from the exterior. The flashing system must be designed as an integral component of the stone/truss with field adjustability from the building interior. Critical areas for attention during detailing, as usual, are the atypical locations such as exterior face of columns, exterior corner faces, flashing of spandrel faces, panel-to-panel flashing connections, and other areas where access from the interior is very limited. It becomes apparent that the performance of the stone/truss wall system is subject to very critical narrow tolerance bands for fabrication and installation, wherein all involved building trades must provide high quality workmanship without undermining the work of others within the system.

Responsibility

To create the authority and responsibility to perform the high quality workmanship required within rather narrow tolerance limitations, all aspects of the stone/truss wall assembly must be delivered as a sole source responsibility by a single major subcontractor. This subcontractor should be responsible for material, system design and fabrication, and installation as well as the proper integration of work by other building trades, such as windows. This single source subcontractor is responsible to provide a long-term warranty/guarantee.

No two projects are exactly the same. All designs can produce anomalies which cannot be predicted on the drawing board, or today, by computer analysis. For these reasons it is vital and prudent to perform a wall mock-up testing program of the stone/truss wall system, at an independent testing laboratory, to evaluate construction techniques, flashing and drainage systems, structural capabilities of the system design, as well as loads produced by contiguous components of the specific project [7]. Only through the use of large-scale wall testing will it be possible to determine if a given wall assembly will satisfy the performance criteria specified for the project and be free of unforeseen problems. Even today, it should be realized that wall construction is an inexact science.

Quality control and quality assurance of the stone/truss wall is of paramount importance if the wall construction is to perform to defined building envelope performance criteria. Performance is judged both in initial testing results and the expectation of continued long-term performance over time.

Other Trades

Though normally not considered a primary concern of the stone work trade, it is important to identify as early as possible in the design process the needs and impact of the other trades which comprise the remaining components of the exterior wall work. Most projects have generous areas of windows in situ to the stone facade which must be integrated into the stonework to produce the complete exterior envelope. As an example, window washing systems can be difficult to integrate into the wall assembly if this selection is postponed until after the start of truss fabrication.

Criteria and considerations for support, imposed loading, corrosion, drainage, etc. for these other components are equal in concern and will impact the overall building envelope performance. Communication between all wall trades is essential at very early stages. Again, the use of a single source subcontractor will aid these efforts and improve the quality of the entire envelope.

Conclusions

Thin-stone wall systems can offer the architect the ability to use stone on his project to satisfy a design when a traditional stone system would be prohibitive. It is important to note, however, that thin stone wall systems are not free from limitations and restrictions, especially thin stone/truss panel walls. Neither can it be said that thin stone/truss conform to the same limitations and restrictions as traditional stone systems. A major caution to the architect/engineer lies in the selected fabricator's in-house "system's engineering" capability. As a comparison, most curtain wall companies provide an "engineered" wall system which addresses the aspects of the aforementioned performance criteria, tailored to the needs of the project. This vital service has not gone without an associated cost, which allows the fabricator to do his "engineering homework" and produce a reliable product in reality as well as on paper. This full service capability is vital to the needs of most building owners, since most owners do not wish to have their project be the first experimental use of a stone contractor's system.

In contrast to those companies specializing in curtain walls, this engineering capability is, sorry to say, lacking in many thin stone/truss contractors. Some stone contractors offer what is promoted to be a wall system, but in reality provides only a rudimentary veneer-cladding system capable of only providing support for the stone veneer without addressing and resolving the needs for water penetration, thermal barrier, window support, etc. Such cladding systems at best should be considered for the least significant projects, since their reduced cost is based upon an incomplete envelope system and provide much divided responsibilities. It should be noted that when responsibilities are divided and the inevitable conflicts arise, the party that all turn to is the architect/engineer, to "engineer" the remedial solutions. With the many new developments in thin-stone technology, it is sufficient to say that the parties with the greatest expertise are the stone fabricators/installers/contractors, not the design professionals. It is therefore important to have on-board a stone contractor with the full range of capabilities consistent with the project requirements.

The use of stone/truss building envelopes can be an integral part of the palette available for use by the architect/engineer, but it is vital to evaluate the specific merits and detractions of a system based upon the established project design criteria for the complete stone assembly. This evaluation will require a comprehensive, not cursory, review of each proposed system to an extent not commonly considered necessary. Industry standards, technical information, and other data to aid in the evaluation process are at best rather sparse and somewhat conflicting. Each component, material, and assembly must be analyzed and evaluated against the present criteria values. This will only then allow evaluation of the expectations of the design versus the capabilities of the selected wall system.

References

[1] Mckee, H. J., "Introduction to Early American Masonry, Stone, Brick, Mortar and Plaster," National Trust for Historic Preservation and Columbia University, New York, July 1973.
[2] "Buildings are Turning to Stone," *Engineering News Record,* 8 March 1984.
[3] ASTM Test Method for Modulus of Rupture of Natural Building Stone (C99).
[4] AAMA: "Structural Properties of Glass," Series No. 12, Architectural Aluminum Manufacturer's Association, Des Plains, IL, 1984.
[5] ASTM Test Method for Structural Performance of Glass in Exterior Windows, Curtain Walls, and Doors Under the Influence of Uniform Static Loads by Destructive Method (E 997).
[6] Skolnik, A. D., "Testing for Acid Rain," *Progressive Architecture,* July 1983.
[7] AAMA 501: "Methods of Test for Metal Curtain Walls," Architectural Aluminum Manufacturer's Association, Des Plains, IL, 1983.

[8] AAMA "Design Windloads for Buildings and Boundary Layer Wind Tunnel Testing," Series No. 11, Architectural Aluminum Manufacturer's Association, Des Plains, IL, 1985.
[9] Horne, T. A., "Corrosion," *AOPA Pilot,* May 1982.
[10] Panek, J. R. and Cook, J. P., *Construction Sealants and Adhesives,* 2nd ed., John Wiley and Sons, New York, 1984.

Truss Supported Stone Panel Systems

Stephen Gulyas[1]

Truss Supported Stone Panel Systems

REFERENCE: Gulyas, S., **"Truss Supported Stone Panel Systems,"** *New Stone Technology, Design, and Construction for Exterior Wall Systems, ASTM STP 996*, B. Donaldson, Ed., American Society for Testing and Materials, Philadelphia, 1988, pp. 69–86.

ABSTRACT: The truss-supported stone panel evolved during the last 20 years from simple strongbacks to entire prefabricated building bays. The advantages of prefabrication assure higher quality at competitive cost. The development of the many types of truss panels was dictated by the various characteristics of specific buildings. These panels can take practically any form, from strongbacks to spandrel and window truss panels, column truss panels, full wall panels, and specials. The panel is assembled with the truss in either vertical or horizontal position. The type of assembly greatly influences the type of stone anchor system to be used. A variety of stone anchor systems have proven value. The steel truss panels themselves need special connections to the supporting building frame to accommodate the various building movements without transferring forces to the truss panel. Design, proper installation, and inspection of such connections are vital. Full-scale mock-ups should be built for testing and feasibility of construction. The possibilities of the prefabricated stone panel systems are great, but they require vigilance and professional planning.

KEY WORDS: stone wall panels, prefabrication, wall panels, stone anchors, wall panel anchors, stone replacement, wall panel assembly, mock-up, testing, truss panels, building movements

Introduction

Prefabrication or panelization of stone cladding was a natural development in creating the exterior envelope of buildings in our technologically advanced age. This development has been gradual. The "exposed aggregate" look on precast concrete panels was replaced with stone on precast concrete. Shortly thereafter, prefabricated steel frame supported stone cladding was developed. This industry is about 20 years old. We have accepted the term "truss supported stone panel systems," which conjures up in our minds the familiar-looking steel truss spanning from column to column with stone panels attached along one side. Though most of the panels look like that, other panels made up of stone on prefabricated steel frames, usually called "strongbacks," do not resemble a truss but are as rigid as a truss.

Significance

The exterior enclosure of buildings has become more complex. High performance is required to protect the structure and its occupants from the elements, at the lowest cost.

Truss panel systems try to meet the challenge by offering the following advantages:

1. *Speedier construction time.* Fabrication of panels may start from the first day of con-

---

[1] Technical director and vice president, Stone Tech, Inc., Long Island City, NY 11101.

struction to provide for faster enclosure of the building, which will allow faster progress of the interior work.

2. *Economy.* Assembly line production assures greater productivity with less expensive shop labor and the elimination of interruptions due to bad weather.

3. *Better quality.* Easier working conditions in the shop will result in better quality than if the same work is performed on a hanging scaffold. Quality control in the shop can be more efficient.

4. *Lighter weight.* Weight is the key issue when comparing the truss panel with the stone-faced precast concrete panel, which can be more than three times the weight of the stone-faced steel truss panel. The resulting savings in framing and foundation cost for a high-rise building can be considerable. The lighter weight may also provide an additional advantage when seismic loading must be considered.

Obviously, all these advantages ultimately can be measured in savings.

Because of the complexity of the exterior enclosure of the building, the close cooperation of various disciplines is required during the development of a project. The owner, the building design team (the architect, the engineer, and a cladding consultant), and the contractor should work together to decide which stone support system is the most desirable for a particular project to fulfill the specified requirements for the exterior enclosure.

There are a number of buildings where the stone support system was changed on the basis of recommendations by the contractor or the cladding design consultant. The Battery Park World Financial Center in New York City, for example, was originally designed with stone-faced precast concrete panels, but during the bidding process the design was changed to a truss-supported stone panel system [1]. A portion of the last building was changed again back to stone-faced precast concrete; all systems were dictated by feasibility and economy. On the other hand, the Lucky Goldstar Headquarter Building in Seoul, South Korea was envisioned by its development architect [2] to have a truss panel system. When the cladding consultant was commissioned to design its cladding it was found that, while a truss panel system was quite possible, field-placed stone slabs on an aluminum mullion system would be more feasible and more economical.

Truss Panel Systems

General

In evaluating what type of truss panel system is most desirable for a particular building, or whether the truss panel system is feasible at all, many items have to be considered:

1. *Architectural configuration of the facade.* What is the shape and degree of repetition of the facade? A simple flat and repetitious facade is most ideally suited for truss panels. A complex project requires extensive lead time for engineering, for coordination with adjoining construction, and for tooling up for the many types of truss panels.

2. *Fenestration.* Are the windows horizontal strips, vertical strips, or individual punch windows? This will generally influence the size and type of truss panels.

3. *Column spacing.* What is the size of the spandrel? This will greatly influence the size and the anchor requirements of the panels. Furthermore, this may also necessitate addition to, or modification of, the building frame, which will add to the cost of the systems.

4. *Limitations on the transportation of the panels.* Underpass and city street restrictions may limit the truss size or may necessitate transportation of the panels in the horizontal position rather than vertically (the position the panels were designed for). Transportation

in the horizontal position can cause shifting of stones and cause many stone anchor failures because of the prying forces created by twisting truck beds. This actually occurred on a New York City project, resulting in extensive repair work at the time of construction and also some years later.

5. *Space limitations at the construction site.* In order to maintain the continuity of the erection process, more than one trailer has to be accommodated at the site. Also, there must be space to accommodate cranes and also room for the panels to go up the side of the building. All this may lead to unresolvable traffic problems. This was one reason the truss panel concept had to be abandoned on a recent New York City project.

Types of Panels

There are a variety of steel truss or steel-framed stone panel systems that have been used over the last two decades. In order to panelize the stone cladding system, one has to bear in mind that horizontal and vertical expansion joints have to be provided to accommodate differential movements between the building's structural frame and the panel. Such movements are accommodated in special panel connections to the building frame. In general the following truss panel systems or combinations of systems exist:

1. *Strongbacks (Fig. 1)* were the first to appear as stone supporting prefabricated steel frame systems. Generally they were vertical panels between windows spanning from floor to floor and replacing the field-applied vertical struts or the masonry wall backup of the stone cladding. In New York City some early examples of these systems were used for the

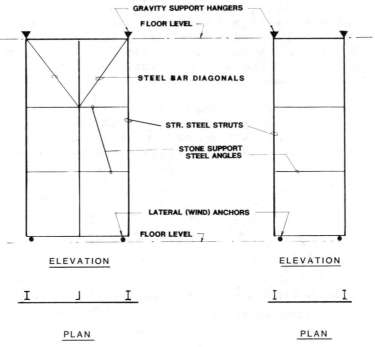

FIG. 1—*Strong back panels.*

Harlem State Office Building [3] and for the New York Telephone Building in Manhattan at 375 Pearl Street [4], among others.

2. *Spandrel truss panel* (*Fig. 2*) is probably the most commonly used stone panel today. Sometimes the panel may also include soffit and sill. Usually the panel is supported on or near the columns to carry the weight of the panel and the weight of the windows and infill panels which are supported on the truss panel. Lateral supports perpendicular to the plane of the wall are applied to the columns and to the floor and spandrel beam to resist against windload. Panels are generally 20 to 30 ft. long, but sometimes can be 40 ft. to reach far-spaced columns. The windows and infill panels span vertically between two spandrel panels. Some examples of this system are the IBM headquarters building in New York City [5], the elliptical building on 53rd at Third Avenue [6] where each truss panel was fabricated in multifaceted segments, and the building at 1333 "H" Street, Washington, DC [7].

3. *Column truss panel* (*Fig. 3*) spans vertically from floor to floor and supports the infill spandrel panel. It is found viable where the columns are close spaced or where the facade has strong vertically running features. An example is 60 State Street in Boston [8], where strong column features necessitated the use of vertical space frame trusses.

4. *Combined spandrell truss panel and window strip truss panel* (*Fig. 4*) are joined to each other on the building after they are erected. The spandrel panel carries its own weight as well as the weight of the window truss panel. The window truss panel is also designed to carry its own weight during handling and transportation, but once in place on top of the spandrel panel the diagonals from the window openings are removed. Vertical members of both panels are then interconnected in order to span vertically between the floors to resist windload. Such a cladding system is used to enclose three of the towers of the World Financial Center at Battery Park.

5. *The full wall panel* (*Fig. 5*) approaches a more ideal condition by prefabricating all wall and window components in a single unit. In this case, the entire wall from floor to floor and column to column (between the horizontal and vertical expansion joints) is prefabricated and erected as one unit. The advantage of prefabrication is further utilized in this system by reducing the number of field connections. This insures better quality control, reduces field labor, and speeds up erection. However, handling and transportation are the limiting factors. Such a system was used for the last building of the World Financial Center at Battery Park [9].

6. *Special types of truss panels and systems* may be developed to suit the unusual geometry created by the architect. Basically, any shape can be prefabricated. The giant columns, including the large column capitals of the building at 40 W. 53rd Street in New York City [10], were prefabricated in 2.3-m-wide octagonal granite-faced drum sections.

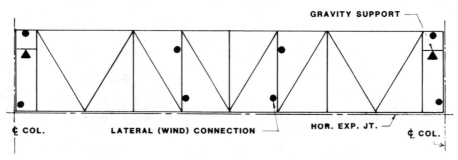

FIG. 2—*Spandrel truss panel.*

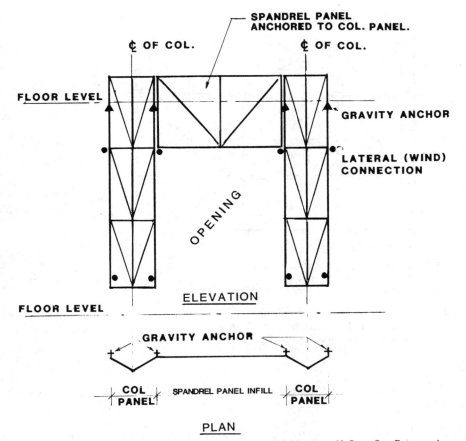

FIG. 3—*Column truss panel with infill spandrel panel (Project: 60 State St., Boston; Architect: Skidmore, Owings & Merrill, Chicago; Cladding design: Stonimpex Inc.).*

7. There are developments at this time toward the prefabrication of stone-supporting aluminum frame systems. The aluminum mullion framing is panelized with the stone and with windows preinstalled in the plant. This is, however, a new generation of prefabricated stone panel systems.

Elements of the Truss Panel (Figs. 6 and 7)

Stone Slabs

Stone slabs or other stone elements can be of any size or configuration. Minimum thickness may be as little as 1 in. if the quality of stone, the windload, the type of anchorage, and the applicable building code allow it. The New York City Building Code specifies the use of minimum 1-5/8-in. stone thickness for the exterior, and application for code variance is required if thinner stone is planned. There are numerous projects in New York City where 1-3/16 in. thickness was allowed after substantiation for the adequacy was provided for each

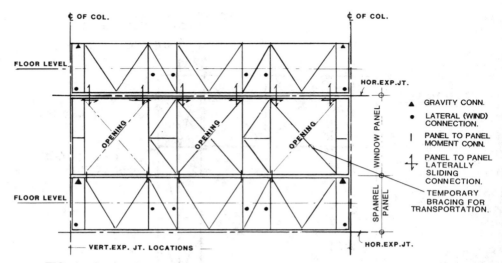

FIG. 4—*Combined spandrel and window strip truss panel (Project: Battery Park World Financial Center, New York City; Architect: Cesar Pelli & Associates/Adamson Associates; Cladding design: FEI Corp./The Office of Irwin G. Cantor, P.C.).*

project. The adequacy had to be substantiated by engineering calculations, physical performance test data, and presentation of existing successfully performing cladding systems having less than 1-5/8-in.-thick stone panels.

Stone Anchors

Anchor types may be divided into two groups according to the method of the truss panel assembly:

1. *Assembly in vertical position (Fig. 6).* Perimeter anchors are used generally when the

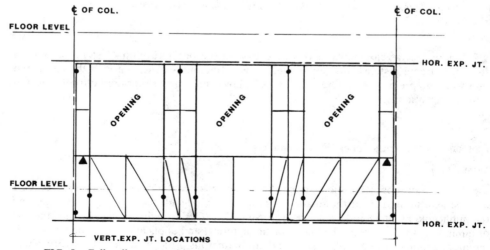

FIG. 5—*Full wall truss panel (Project: Battery Pack World Financial Center, "B" Building, New York City; Architect: Cesar Pelli & Associates/Haines Lundberg Waehler; Cladding design: Artex Precast Ltd., Concord, Ont.).*

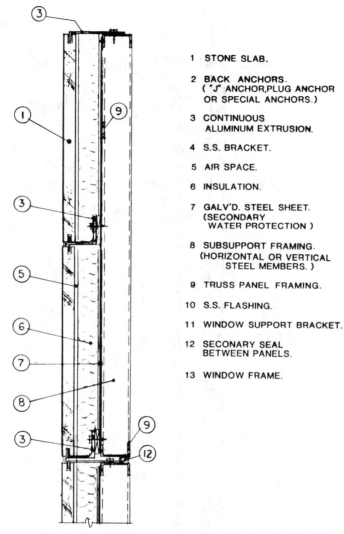

1 STONE SLAB.

2 BACK ANCHORS.
   ("J" ANCHOR, PLUG ANCHOR
   OR SPECIAL ANCHORS.)

3 CONTINUOUS
   ALUMINUM EXTRUSION.

4 S.S. BRACKET.

5 AIR SPACE.

6 INSULATION.

7 GALV'D. STEEL SHEET.
   (SECONDARY
      WATER PROTECTION)

8 SUBSUPPORT FRAMING.
   (HORIZONTAL OR VERTICAL
         STEEL MEMBERS.)

9 TRUSS PANEL FRAMING.

10 S.S. FLASHING.

11 WINDOW SUPPORT BRACKET.

12 SECONARY SEAL
    BETWEEN PANELS.

13 WINDOW FRAME.

FIG. 6—*Panel assembled in vertical position (see also Fig. 11).*

panel is assembled in the vertical position—the same position it will occupy on the building. In this case the weight of the stone slabs is usually supported along their bottom edge by a plate, an angle, or an aluminum extrusion. These supports could also provide lateral anchorage by a welded lug, loose dowel, or an appropriate extrusion which fits into a kerf made in the edge of the stone slabs. If individual lateral anchors, like strap or rod anchors, are used, they will be placed along the side edges of the stone slab.

Anchors embedded in the backside of the stone panels could also be used when the panel assembly is performed in the vertical position. Figure 8 shows such a three-way adjustable anchor.

2. *Assembly in horizontal position (Fig. 7).* When the assembly is made by having the panel in the horizontal position on an assembly table, where the stone slabs are laid out

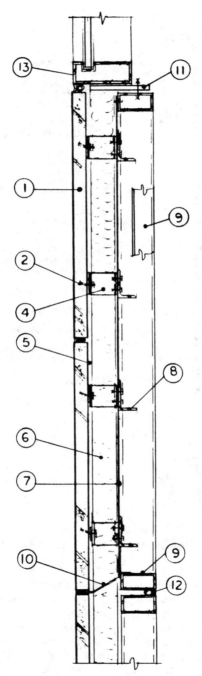

FIG. 7—*Panel assembled in horizontal position (see Fig. 6 for interpretation of numbers).*

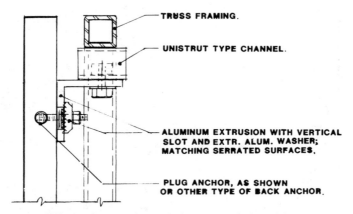

FIG. 8—*Stone anchor with three ways of adjustability.*

first with their finished face down, the anchors are usually embedded in the back side of the stone slab. These are special rod anchors embedded in specially fabricated holes or slots in the back of the stone. They all should have the ability to mechanically anchor the stone by providing some sort of "lock-in" wedge action. The anchor should not rely solely on the performance of structural adhesives like epoxies or polyester resins. (It is not stated here that the adhesives are unreliable, but certain authorities with jurisdiction, like the New York City Building Department, at the most recent time do not consider them as having proven long-time performance and accept them only as a filler material.) The anchor system should perform without relying on the adhesive quality of these materials, and tests should be conducted to substantiate this. There is no current standard for safety factors of such stone anchors, but it is recommended here that an epoxied anchor should have a minimum safety factor of 6 as installed, and at least 2 when the adhesive quality of the fillers are discounted. (This is not to be understood to mean that anchors installed without epoxy may have a safety factor as low as 2.)

Some varieties of back anchors in common use are shown in Fig. 9. There are other anchors developed with the same common goal of mechanically locking the anchor within the stone, but they are proprietary items of fabricators and therefore are not shown here.

In the development of an anchor system it should be kept in mind that the stone slab is rigid and that the backup truss frame has a certain elasticity. During handling, transportation, and erection the truss frame has the tendency to deflect, warp, and twist out of plane. This is especially true with longer trusses. The stone slabs through their anchors tend to resist these movements. In order to prevent the development of prying and large forces in the anchors, which could lead to stone breakage, careful handling of the panels is required. Either a more rigid panel backup frame or an anchor system which does not resist the movements of the panel frame but which allows minute movements itself is preferred.

All anchors and anchor components which are embedded in or are in contact with the stone should be of stainless steel type 300 series. Extruded aluminum may be used, but in contact with limestone a protective coating is recommended. Extruded aluminum placed in a stone kerf filled with sealant which is compatible with the stone joint sealant is considered to be adequately protected.

Special attention should be given to the prevention of electrochemical reaction between different metals. All components of the stone anchor assembly, including washers, should be made of stainless steel. Washers may also be made of plastic or neoprene.

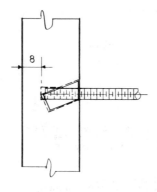

PLUG WITH THREADED ROD ANCHOR

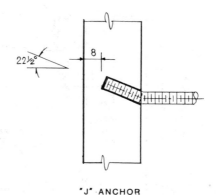

"J" ANCHOR

BENT THREADED ROD EPOXIED INTO STONE

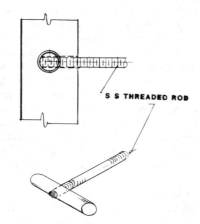

PLUG WITH THREADED ROD ANCHOR
FOR EDGE OF STONE

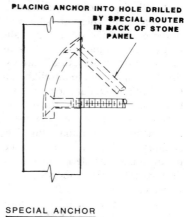

SPECIAL ANCHOR
BY COLD SPRING GRANITE CO.

FIG. 9—*Stone slab back anchors.*

Stone Replacement

Regardless of what type of anchor system is selected for the stone slabs, a method of replacing broken or rejected stone slabs always has to be developed. After the truss panel is erected on the building, the anchor system for stone replacement can rarely be the same as the original system. An anchoring method for stone replacement should be designed, and it should be included in the shop drawings of the panel system. However, experience shows that usually the need for such details is recognized only as an afterthought, and sometimes the result is an awkward design of questionable value. Such a detail where bolting through the stone was used, the nut was recessed in the stone and the hole patched with epoxy or a stone plug. Many of these patches were noticeable, and after the epoxy shrunk and they were subjected to freeze-thaw cycles, some became dislodged. Figure 10 shows a system which was developed by Stone Tech, Inc. and which was used successfully on some of the buildings of Battery Park World Financial Center. The system can be adopted to practically any truss panel system regardless of the original stone anchors.

Water Protection

Stone joints should be sealed with appropriate sealants, preferably in the truss assembly plant. Secondary water protection is recommended to collect moisture due to sealant failure and condensation. Usually the system is part of the panel assembly. It could be a continuous galvanized or stainless steel sheet with appropriate weeps and flashing, a backup gutter system with weeps or drain tubes directing the water into vertical mullions.

Insulation

Therma insulation, if possible, should be part of the panel system in order to assure the proper continuity and the quality workmanship which could be compromised many times if field applied. It should be assured that all steel members which could conduct heat to the outside receive adequate and uniform insulation coverage.

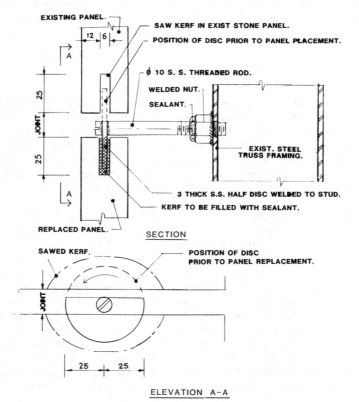

FIG. 10—*Lateral (wind) anchor detail for replacement stone slab* (*Cladding consultant: Stone Tech, Inc.*).

Insulation should be of nonorganic material which does not absorb or hold water. It should not be in direct contact with the stone in order to assure air circulation. In case of direct contact the insulation prevents uniform drying of the stone after rain and could cause its surface to appear blotchy.

Design of Truss Panel Framing and Connections

Truss Panel Frame

Truss panel framing is made up of steel members welded together to form a wall panel rigid in its plane. The panel has to be rigid in order not to transfer forces to the stone anchors. Vertical deflection of the truss is usually negligible, but if it would have an undesirable effect on the panel joints, the stone slabs may be assembled in such a way that when the panel is erected on the building all the joints are straight and uniform. The frame members can be wide flange beams, channels, angles, tubes, bent plates, or cold-formed heavy gage galvanized steel sections such as C studs and joists. Diagonal members may be angles, rods, or straps. Properly designed steel sheet, also used as a secondary water protection, may also serve as truss diagonals. The design may be done routinely by following basic structural engineering principles.

However, the panel connections to the building are usually special connections at the interface between the panel and the building; such connections require special attention in design and construction to assure proper functioning and long-term performance. Steel members should be galvanized or should receive a high-grade protective coating (coal tar epoxy, etc.).

Panel Connections

As stated before, the panel frames are rigid in the plane of the wall. The building frames, however, are subjected to movements. Connections of the truss cladding panels to the building structure have to be able to accommodate all these movements to assure that no loads are transferred to the panel. If the truss panel were rigidly anchored to the building frame the movements would generate huge forces in the panel connections which could cause buckling of panel-framing members, failure of the stone anchors, or breakage of the stone slabs. Movements which must be accounted for in the connections are:

1. *Building sway.* Generally caused by wind and rarely by earthquake. The sway, also known as parallelograming of the frame, could be as much as 1/500 of the height by code allowance which is about 5/16 in. per floor. Figure 11 shows the relationship of the swayed building frame and the rigid wall panel.

2. *Concrete column shortenings.* Caused by long-term shrinkage and creep under load.

3. *Deflection of spandrel beams under floor live load and long-term deflection of concrete spandrel beams.* Cantilevered floor areas are especially vulnerable to deflections and should be given special attention for their effect on the wall panel system. Particular attention should be paid when large cantilevered building frames support several floor levels. As the erection of the panels progresses upward, the deflection of the cantilever increases, and this could cause unexpected stresses in the connections of the earlier-placed panels.

4. *Differential thermal movements between the building frame and the panel framing.* This happens when the insulation is located on the inside face of the panel framing.

Figure 11 indicates the freedom of movements which should be provided for in the various panel connections.

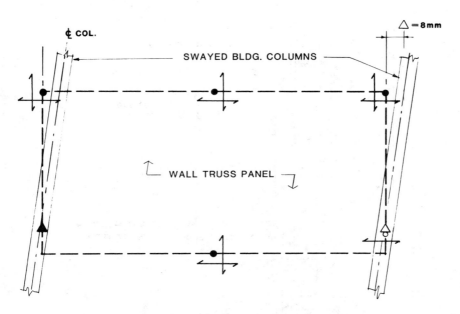

**ARROWS DENOTE PROVISIONS FOR MOVEMENT
IN THE PANEL TO BUILDING CONNECTIONS.**

FIG. 11—*Freedom of movements of typical building panel connections.*

Two load-bearing connections support the truss panel and maintain the horizontal expansion joints. One of the two bearing connections should be fixed in all directions in order
to prevent the panel from creeping along the support because of thermal movements and
vibration. The other bearing connection should allow movement in the horizontal plane of
the wall. All other connections should allow movements in both horizontal and vertical
directions in the plane of the wall.

The bearing connections should be located on or near the columns where deflection of
the support points would be negligible. Usually brackets to the columns are provided for
the panel bearing. The desired fixity of one of the bearing connections could be provided
by welding or by providing another movement limiting anchor near the bearing point. Lateral
connections are usually applied at the floor level or to the web or to the bottom flange of
the spandrel beam. In case of no spandrel beam, such as concrete flat plate construction,
lateral support may be provided by a diagonal brace above the ceiling line to the bottom
of the floor slab. Diagonal bracing may also be required if a connection to the bottom flange
of the spandrel beam would cause unacceptable torsion in the spandrel beam.

Where columns are closely spaced (such as in "tubular" frame design) the spandrel or
wall panel could be designed to span horizontally between columns without having intermediate lateral anchors.

Lateral connections should be designed and detailed to allow for sideway movements
indicated in the diagram (Fig. 11). The desired movements may be assured by providing
slotted holes with low friction contact surfaces. Teflon-coated or stainless steel shims and
washers have been used for this purpose. Bolt jamming or loosening should be prevented
by locking the nuts in proper locations using double nuts or nylock nuts. Threaded rod
anchors of sufficient lengths to provide for lateral flexibility are also used to allow sideway
movement. Figure 12 shows another type of lateral anchor which was used on 1333 "H"
Street in Washington, DC.

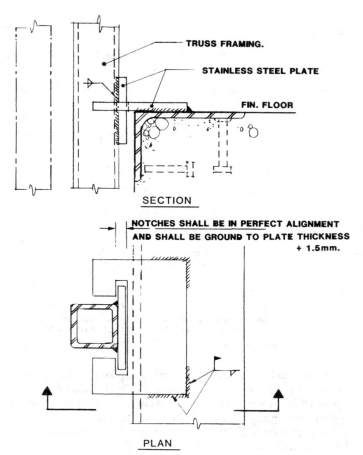

SECTION

NOTCHES SHALL BE IN PERFECT ALIGNMENT
AND SHALL BE GROUND TO PLATE THICKNESS
+ 1.5mm.

TRUSS FRAMING.

STAINLESS STEEL PLATE

FIN. FLOOR

PLAN

FIG. 12—*Truss lateral anchor with two-way freedom of movements (Project: 1333 H Street, Washington, DC; Cladding design: Stephen Gulyas, P.E.).*

Erection Tolerances

Connections should be designed to have ample adjustability. It is not sufficient to provide adjustment capability to accommodate only the "allowable" tolerances specified for steel or concrete construction. Experience shows that building frames, components, inserts, weld-plates, etc. are often not located within the specified tolerances. The connections with inadequate adjustability sometimes are corrected by "field fittings" without proper engineering control. Field fitting is done in the name of expediency because "the next panel is already lifted by the crane" or "the truck has to be unloaded" or "the next trade is close behind," etc. A minimum of 2-in. horizontal adjustability is recommended, 1 in. in each direction. In the vertical dimension usually lesser tolerances are adequate, such as a recommended minimum of 1/2 in. up and 1/2 in. down. Each element of the connection should be designed for its worst condition where the combination of factors will result in the largest loads and stresses.

Reliability of the vertical adjustment of load-bearing connections is very important in order to maintain the effective depth of the horizontal expansion joint. Fixed shims, ad-

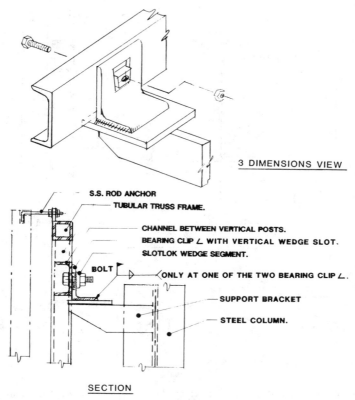

3 DIMENSIONS VIEW

S.S. ROD ANCHOR

TUBULAR TRUSS FRAME.

CHANNEL BETWEEN VERTICAL POSTS.
BEARING CLIP ∟ WITH VERTICAL WEDGE SLOT.
SLOTLOK WEDGE SEGMENT.

BOLT

ONLY AT ONE OF THE TWO BEARING CLIP ∟.

SUPPORT BRACKET

STEEL COLUMN.

SECTION

FIG. 13—*Truss panel bearing connection.*

justable wedge anchor (Fig. 13), or threaded vertical studs with adjustable nuts (Fig. 14) are preferred choices in controlling adjustment. Slotted connections which depend on torquing bolts to prevent slippage are discouraged because they may slip. While high-strength bolts perform well for erection of the building frame, there is not sufficient assurance that the high-strength bolts used in conjunction with truss panels will be properly torqued in every instance. It is necessary to keep in mind that field conditions and personnel involved with panel installation are totally different from those of a structural steel installation.

Some examples of successful methods for anchor adjustment are illustrated by the following jobs: Wedge type connections performed very well in the erection of the truss panels on the Battery Park Financial Center project (Fig. 13); vertical-threaded stud welded to a bearing plate that swivels provided a very versatile three-way adjustment for the bearing connections of the 1333 "H" Street project in Washington, DC. (Fig. 14).

There have been many kinds of connections used with truss panels, but in all cases the "rule" of their design should be *simplicity*. A crane should be able to place a panel on two load-bearing connections which can be easily adjusted in all directions. Panels should be temporarily secured with some of the lateral connections to free the crane for the next panel lift. Before the next panel arrives, the erection crew has to install all lateral anchors and do final adjustments. Welded connections should have erection bolts or other means to permit subsequent organized welding operations.

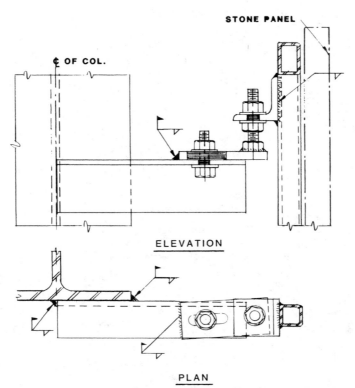

FIG. 14—*Truss panel bearing connection (Project: 1333 H Street, Washington, DC; Architect: Skidmore, Owings & Merrill, Washington, DC; Cladding design: Stephen Gulyas, P.E.).*

Panel Assembly

The method of panel assembly is basically determined by the type of stone anchor system used or vice versa; the stone anchor system is determined by the method of assembly which the panel fabricator is equipped to do. There are two basic assembly methods:

Vertical Position

Stone slabs that are supported along their periphery, mostly at the top and bottom kerfs, are assembled in the plant by having the steel truss in the *vertical position*. The setting of the stone slabs will be as if it were being done on the side of the building, except that it can be done in a highly organized assembly line method. The advantage of this method is that all adjustments can be made so that all stone slabs are in alignment and in plumb, and that the panel can be handled in the vertical position from fabrication to erection.

Horizontal Position

When back anchors are used for suspension of the stone slabs the assembly usually takes place in the *horizontal position*, similar to the manufacturing of stone-faced precast concrete panels. In this case the assembly line could also include the fabrication of the steel trusses.

At first, the stone slabs are laid out on the assembly table having spacers between the joints to maintain the proper size. Depending on the assembly detail, the anchor holes are either predrilled or drilled on the assembly table at the exactly laid out locations. Stone anchors are placed into the holes and carefully lined in the vertical position. If insulation is specified to be between the stone and the truss frame, special steel brackets or other provisions are applied onto the protruding stone anchors. The purpose of the brackets is to act as spacers between the back of the stone and the truss frame. They are actually little cantilevered support brackets that anchor the stone off the truss frames once the panel is in the vertical position. The brackets are carefully leveled on the assembly table to receive the prefabricated steel frame. The steel frame is lowered in horizontal position, assuring that the stone anchors protrude through the anchor holes which are provided in the steel frame. If insulation is used between the stone and the truss panel, it should be placed on spacers on top of the stone prior to lowering the truss frame. The spacers could be strips of rubber which are withdrawn after the insulation is secured in place.

After the truss frame is lowered, nuts are applied onto the protruding stone anchors to secure them to the truss frame. Prior to placing the nuts it is important that the steel frame is brought in direct contact with the stone anchor brackets to assure that the nuts can be installed without applying pullout load on the stone anchors, since that may damage the stone. After the assembly the panels are brought into upright position for further handling. The truss panels have to be designed with appropriate provisions provided for this maneuver in order to prevent damaging the stone.

There are variations on the assembly procedures of certain items, depending on the system developed by the various fabricators.

Joint sealant can be applied to the panels in the fabricator's plant instead of on the building for better quality control and economy. In that case the panels are stored until the sealant is adequately cured before shipment.

Testing

The performance of a truss panel system, like other cladding systems, should be verified by full-scale mock-up testing unless the project is very small and it is not feasible economically. The truss panels may be only part of the cladding mock-up. The tests are to prove that the proposed system will adequately meet the specified requirements for air infiltration, static and dynamic water infiltration, and positive and negative wind load. Thermal and seismic effect and the effect of lateral sway on the stone and panel connections could also be tested if required. Generally the panel system is tested to 1.5 times the design load. This test, however, is not considered adequate for proving the performance of an individual stone slab. The individual stone slab and its anchor system can be tested to a higher safety factor by building a small wood chamber around the designated stone slab and pumping air out of the chamber to create a suction force until failure occurs in the stone slab or its anchor provisions. It is generally desired that no failure should take place until four times the design load is reached.

Deflections of the panel system are also recorded in order to assure that they remain below the specified allowable deflection, usually L/240 or less without permanent set in any of the components.

The mock-up is usually built by the cladding contractor at a rented laboratory facility. Constructing the mock-up is found very useful for the contractor in order to familiarize himself with the system and to eliminate trouble spots and possible interface problems with other trades (windows, waterproofing, etc). For his erection work he should develop a meaningful self-imposed quality control program.

After the construction of the cladding work is progressing, additional tests in the field may be performed on the actual panel to verify that the routine field installation can also meet the specified requirements.

Inspection

The proper performance of the exterior enclosure is vital to the use of present day buildings. Having a part or the entire system prefabricated in a shop, it is prudent to have it done under a continuous quality assurance program. A full-time inspector should be employed by, preferably, the project owner or developer. He is to oversee and assure that the fabricator organizes and maintains his own quality assurance program for every item and the assembly of the system.

Conclusion

Prefabrication of the exterior enclosure of buildings is becoming more and more a necessity. The stone-faced steel truss panel has a very important role in this development. New fabrication plants are being built rapidly, and other plants are retooling to produce a more competitive, improved version of the system. The possibilities are great and so should be our vigilance. Intelligent planning with the early involvement of the design team is a must.

References

[1] Design Architect: Cesar Pelli and Associates
    Architect: Adamson Associates
    Cladding Design: FEI Corporation, and The Office of Irwin Cantor
[2] Architect: Skidmore, Owings & Merrill of Chicago
    Cladding Design: Stone Tech, Inc., and Flour City Architectural Metals Corp.
[3] Architect: Ifill-Johnson-Hanchard
    Cladding Design: Joseph Weiss & Sons
[4] Architect: Rose, Beaton & Rose, Architects & Engineers
    Cladding Design: Rose, Beaton & Rose
[5] Architect: Edward L. Barnes, Associates
    Cladding Design: Stephen Gulyas, P.E.
[6] Architect: John Burgee and Phillip H. Johnson
    Cladding Design: Curtainwall Design Consultants.
[7] Architect: Skidmore, Owings and Merrill of Washington[8]
    Cladding Design: Stephen Gulyas, P.E.
[8] Architect: Skidmore, Owings & Merrill of Chicago
    Cladding Design: Stonimpax
[9] Design Architect: Cesar Pelli and Associates
    Architect: Haines Lundberg Waehler
    Cladding Design: Artex Precast, Ltd.
[10] Architect: Kevin Roche, John Dinkeloo and Associates
    Stone Cladding Design: Stone Tech, Inc., and Curtainwall Design Consultants

Precast Concrete and Fiberglass Reinforced Cement (GFRC) Stone Panel Systems

Sidney Freedman[1]

Stone Veneer-Faced Precast Concrete Panels

REFERENCE: Freedman, S., **"Stone Veneer-Faced Precast Concrete Panels,"** *New Stone Technology, Design, and Construction for Exterior Wall Systems, ASTM STP 996*, B. Donaldson, Ed., American Society for Testing and Materials, Philadelphia, 1988, pp. 89–104.

ABSTRACT: In the 1960s, the use of stone veneer-faced precast concrete panels became prevalent. As stone veneer becomes thinner, greater emphasis on stone physical properties becomes important as well as examination of factors of safety. A survey of precast concrete panel producers revealed excellent performance of thin stone veneers over the last 20 years.
   The precast concrete industry recommends that there be no concrete bonding between stone veneer and concrete backup in order to eliminate bowing, cracking, and staining of the veneer. Mechanical anchors should be used to secure the veneer.

KEY WORDS: anchorage, anchor holes, bond breakers, caulking, cleaning, epoxy, finish, freeze-thaw, granite, jointing, limestone, marble, natural stone, panels, permeability, precast concrete, properties, repair, responsibilities, safety factors, samples, sandwich panels, shear capacity, shop drawings, sizes, thickness, tolerances, travertine, veneer-faced precast concrete, volume change, watertightness, weathering

Natural stone has been widely used in building construction for centuries due to its strength, durability, aesthetic effect, availability, and inherent low maintenance costs. Originally utilized as a load-bearing structural material, natural stone began to receive attention in veneer or skin applications with the advent of the skeleton frame type of buildings. In the 1960s, the practice of facing buildings with large prefabricated concrete components to decrease construction time and reduce costs resulted in combining the rich beauty of natural stone with the strength, versatility, and economy of precast concrete.

Some of the advantages of stone veneer-faced precast concrete panels are: (1) veneer stock can be used in thin sections because of shorter spans between anchoring points; (2) multiplane units such as column covers, spandrels with integral soffit and sill sections, deep reveal window frames, inside and outside corners, projections and setbacks, and parapet sections are more economically assembled as veneer units on precast panels (Fig. 1); (3) the erection of the precast units is faster and more economical than conventional hand-set construction because the larger panels incorporate a number of veneer pieces; and (4) the veneered concrete panels can be used to span column to column, thereby reducing floor edge loading. Spandrel panels have been as large as 6 by 43 ft (1.8 by 13.1 m) and 8 by 35 ft (2.4 by 10.7 m), while a single story panel has typically been 13 to 30 ft (4.0 by 9.1 m) by story height.

The use of thin stone veneers on precast panels for high-rise buildings is relatively new, and thus their long-term performance has not been established as has the use of thicker

[1] Director, Architectural Precast Concrete Services, Prestressed Concrete Institute, Chicago, IL 60604.

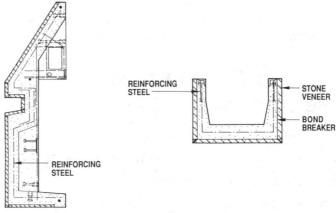

FIG. 1—*Typical spandrel and column cover panels.*

stone veneers. Careful attention is therefore advised in ensuring the necessary strength and serviceability requirements, with particular attention paid to the physical properties of the stone, anchorage of the stone to the concrete, safety factors, and effect of finishes on the strength of the stone.

General Considerations

Structural design, fabrication, handling, and erection considerations for veneered precast concrete units are similar to those for other precast concrete wall panels, except that special consideration must be given to the veneer material and its attachment to the concrete. The physical properties of the stone facing material must be compared with the properties of the concrete backup. These properties include:

1. Tensile (axial and flexural), compressive, and shear strength.
2. Modulus of elasticity (axial tension, flexure, and axial compression).
3. Coefficient of thermal expansion.
4. Volume change.

In evaluating properties of stone, it should be recognized that some natural stones exhibit different properties in different directions. Also, there may be considerable variation in a given direction for different samples of the same stone. The strengths of thin sections of stone are generally more sensitive than thicker sections to imperfections and inclusions of minerals. Also, a stone that has a crystalline structure with dimensions large enough to approach the thickness of the slab itself will be substantially weakened.

Reinforcement of the precast concrete backup should follow recommendations for precast concrete wall panels relative to design, cover, and placement [1]. Cover depth of reinforcement must be a minimum of 1/2 in. (13 mm) at the veneer surface. This cover is maintained by noncorrosive spacers, such as plastic and occasionally concrete or stone. Galvanized or epoxy-coated reinforcement is recommended at cover depths of less than 3/4 in. (19 mm).

Prestressing of panels has been employed on several projects and has been effective in controlling bowing of long, flat, relatively thin panels [2]. Such panels are generally more susceptible to bowing. As with any multilayer panel, trial runs may be necessary to verify an analysis as to the best prestressing strand location in order to avoid an increase in bowing.

Because of the difference in material properties between natural stone and concrete, veneered panels are more susceptible to bowing than all-concrete units. However, panel manufacturers have developed design and production procedures to minimize bowing. Many manufacturers compensate by using cambered forms, for example, 1 in. for 40 ft (25 mm for 12.2 m), to produce panels initially bowed inward. Bowing is also a consideration in reinforcement design. If thickness is sufficient, two layers of reinforcement should be used, as this helps to reduce bowing caused by differential shrinkage or temperature changes. In some cases, reinforcing trusses are used to add stiffness; in others, concrete ribs are formed on the back of the panel, but this may require backforming and is more costly. Minimum thickness of backup concrete of flat panels to control bowing or warping is usually 5 to 6 in. (13 to 15 cm), but 4 in. (10 cm) has been used where the panel is small or it has adequate rigidity obtained through panel shape or thickness of natural stone.

The method of attachment of facing materials should include consideration of factors such as:

1. Shrinkage of concrete during curing.
2. Stresses imposed during handling, transport, and erection.
3. Response to different coefficients of thermal expansion and to thermal gradients (constant interior temperature versus widely varying exterior temperatures) or location of insulation, if any, that is, whether veneer is separated from supporting concrete by insulation and/or bondbreaker, or attached to the exterior wythe of a composite or noncomposite sandwich panel.
4. Service loads.

Concrete, after initial set, begins to shrink as it loses excess water to the surrounding environment. The stone veneer, especially with an impermeable bond breaker, limits drying on the veneered side of the backup concrete. The resulting differential shrinkage of the concrete can cause outward bowing or separation in a simple span panel. The flat surfaces of cut stone reveal bowing much more prominently than all-concrete panels. For this reason, the extent of bowing should be carefully considered even though the rigidity of the cut stone and steel reinforcing may sometimes help to resist bowing. Midpoint tieback connections can help minimize convex bowing.

Cracking in the veneer may occur if the bonding or anchoring details force the veneer pieces to follow the bowing. This could be critical where the individual stone pieces are large and/or the veneer is thin, and the concrete shrinkage is significant. Control of concrete shrinkage necessitates close attention to concrete mix design, continuous control of water and cement content in the mix, and prolonged curing under proper humidity conditions or the use of curing compounds on all exposed concrete surfaces, for example, back surface and panel edges.

While all-concrete panels usually bow in response to thermal gradients through the panel thickness, stone-veneered concrete may also bow when the temperature is uniform through the panel thickness. This bowing is caused by differences in the coefficients of expansion of the stone and the concrete. Limestone has an average coefficient of expansion of 2.8×10^{-6} in./in./°F (5.0×10^{-6} mm/mm/°C), while granite has 4.5×10^{-6} (8.1×10^{-6}) and marble 7.3×10^{-6} (13.1×10^{-6}). Coefficients of 6×10^{-6} in./in./°F (10.8×10^{-6} mm/mm/°C) for normal weight and 5×10^{-6} (9.0×10^{-6}) for sand-lightweight concrete are frequently used. As stone becomes thinner, coefficient of expansion differentials become more important because the stone has less rigidity to resist bowing. If the facing stone has a higher coefficient of expansion than the concrete, stresses and deformations in the panel under decreasing temperature will be the reverse of those due to shrinkage. For rising temperatures, the stresses and deformations will be added to that of shrinkage. The reverse situation exists for conditions where the coefficient of expansion of the stone is less than that of the concrete. It is desirable, therefore, to have a backup concrete with low shrinkage and a thermal expansion coefficient that closely approximates that of the stone veneer. The coefficient of thermal expansion of concrete can be varied by changing aggregate type.

Even with the concrete shrinkage kept low, there is still some interaction with the facing material through either adhesive bond or the mechanical anchors. This interaction is minimized by the use of a bond breaker between the facing material and the concrete. Connections of natural stone to the concrete are made with flexible mechanical anchors which can accommodate some relative in-plane movement, a necessity if bond breakers are used. Exceptions are the limestone industry, which, for thick stones, uses rigid rather than flexible anchors and bonds the stone to the concrete, and the fabricators of Danby (calcite) marble, who have recommended flexible anchors and bonding to the concrete.

Panel design must also include "in-service" requirements—in other words, the conditions that panels will encounter when in final location in the structure and subject to the wide range of seasonal and daily temperatures. Generally the interior surfaces of panels are subjected to a very small temperature range, while the exterior surfaces may be exposed to a large daily or seasonal range. The panel manufacturer and designer should consider the following in design and production in order to minimize or eliminate panel bowing:

1. The temperature differential (exterior to interior).
2. Coefficients of expansion of the materials.
3. Ratio of cross-sectional areas of the materials and their moduli of elasticity.
4. Amount, location, and type of reinforcement in the concrete panel.
5. The use of prestressing.
6. Type and location of connections to the structure.
7. Rigidity of connection between stone veneer and concrete backup (too rigid may cause problems).
8. Shrinkage of the concrete.

Since cut stones can be stained by oil and rust, the forms for the precast concrete should be lined with polyethylene sheets or other nonstaining materials. If specifications dictate that the concrete be bonded directly to the veneer in addition to the mechanical anchors, for example, for thick limestone, it is desirable to use a moisture barrier/bonding agent on the back side of the stone to eliminate the possibility of alkali salts in concrete staining the stone veneer. Moisture barrier/bonding agent materials include portland cement containing less than 0.03% water soluble alkalies, waterproof cementitious stone backing, nonstaining asphaltic or bituminous dampproofing, or an epoxy bonding agent that cures in the presence of moisture.

Responsibilities

A survey of precast concrete producers indicates that a developing practice is for the stone supplier or fabricator to sell the stone directly to the general contractor (GC) or the owner [2]. In the past, a stone broker or quarrier coordinated shipment, did stone drawings and cut sheets, drilled anchor holes, and in general handled all problems associated with the manufacturing of the stone. The GC usually has minimal experience in coordinating a stone veneer precast concrete panel job and usually wants the precast concrete supplier to accept responsibility for any and all problems with the stone supplier. However, the precast producer has no contractual control of the stone supplier's actions when the stone is being furnished to him by the owner or GC.

As a standard practice, it is recommended that someone qualified be engaged by the purchaser of the stone to be responsible for the coordination, which includes delivery and scheduling responsibility as well as ensuring acceptable color uniformity.

Coordination should be written into the specifications so its cost can be bid. Frequent visits to the stone fabricator's plant may be required. With proper coordination and advance planning, fabrication and shipments will proceed smoothly. When communication is lacking, major problems in scheduling and delivery may occur.

For larger projects and when feasible, color control or blending for uniformity should be done in the stone fabricator's plant, since ranges of color and shade, finishes, and markings such as veining, seams, and intrusions are easily seen during the finishing stages. Acceptable color of the stone should be judged for an entire building elevation rather than for an individual panel. Also, testing to determine the physical properties of the stone veneer at the design thickness should be conducted by the owner prior to the award of the precast concrete contract to reduce the need for potentially costly repairs or replacement should deficiencies in the stone veneer be found after start of fabrication.

The stone pieces should be marked for panel location at the stone fabricator's plant. The precast concrete producer must provide the GC with stone quantity and sequence requirements to meet the erection sequences which are determined by mutual agreement. For reasons of production efficiency some concrete panels may be produced out of sequence relative to erection sequence. The precast concrete producer and stone fabricator should coordinate packaging requirements to minimize handling and breakage. Extra stone (approximately 2 to 5%) should be supplied to the precast producer to allow immediate replacement of damaged stone pieces, particularly if the stone is not supplied from a domestic source. Deliveries should be scheduled as closely as possible to actual fabriaction schedules.

The responsibility for determining the type of anchorage between the stone and concrete backup varies on different projects [2]. The stone fabricator or concrete precaster appear to have the dominant responsibility for conducting the anchor tests, with the architect or engineer of record occasionally determining the type of anchorage. However, it is preferable for the architect to determine anchor spacing so that common information can be supplied to all bidders. Contract documents should clearly define who drills the anchor holes in the stone; type, number, and location of anchors; and who supplies the anchors. In most cases, the stone fabricator drills the anchor holes in the stone.

Samples

Samples and mock-up units are particularly important for evaluating stone finishes and acceptable color variations.

There is now a good background of experience in the production and erection of stone veneer-faced precast concrete panels. However, it is recommended that, for new and major applications, full-scale mock-up units be manufactured to check out the feasibility of the production and erection process. Tests on sample panels should be made to confirm the suitability of the stone and anchors and the effects of bowing on the panel's performance. Tests on the behavior of the unit for anticipated temperature changes may be required. Mock-ups should be built to test wall, window, and joint performance under the most severe wind and rain conditions. Acceptance criteria for the stone as well as the anchorage should be established in the project specifications.

Shop Drawings

Because of the need for close coordination between the precast manufacturer and stone veneer supplier, shop drawing preparation and submissions may vary from procedures established for nonveneered precast panels. It is suggested that the precast manufacturer detail all precast units to the point where the fabricator of the veneer is able to incorporate details, sizes, and anchor holes for the individual stone pieces.

Checking and approval of these details and shop drawings will be simplified and expedited if they can be combined and/or submitted simultaneously. Separate subcontracts and advance awards often occur in projects with stone-veneered panels. While these procedures may affect normal submission routines, it is not intended that responsibilities for accuracy be transferred or reassigned. In other words, the precast manufacturer is responsible for precast concrete details and dimensions and the stone veneer fabricator is responsible for stone details and dimensions.

The manufacture of stone veneer panels requires adequate lead time in order to avoid construction delays. Therefore, it is important that shop drawing approvals be obtained expeditiously. Furthermore, it is recommended that the designer allow the submission of shop drawings in predetermined stages to allow the start of manufacturing as soon as possible and ensure a steady and timely flow of approved information to allow for uninterrupted fabrication.

Stone Properties

Stone is a product of nature and does not always demonstrate consistent behavior that may apply to manufactured building materials, such as concrete. The strength of natural stone depends on several factors: the size, rift, and cleavage of crystals, the degree of cohesion, the interlocking geometry of crystals, and the nature of natural cementing materials present. The properties of the stone will vary with the locality from which it is quarried. Sedimentary and metamorphic rocks such as limestone and marble will exhibit different strengths when measured parallel and perpendicular to their original bedding planes. Igneous rocks such as granite may exhibit relatively uniform strength characteristics on the various planes. In addition, the surface finish, freezing and thawing, and large temperature fluctuations will affect the strength and, in turn, influence the anchorage system.

To the degree possible, information on the durability of the specified stone should be obtained from the supplier or from observations of existing installations of that particular stone. This information should include such factors as tendency to warp, reaction to weathering forces, resistance to chemical pollutants, resistance to chemical reaction from adjacent materials, and reduction in strength from the effects of weathering.

Prior to the final design of stone veneers, the designer should be involved in determining the tests to be performed to determine the physical properties of the stone being considered. The testing should be done on stone with the same finish and thickness as will be used on the structure. An adequate number of test samples should be selected, and statistical methods should be used to evaluate the physical properties and obtain design values. These properties, along with properties of the anchor system, should be used to assure adequate strength of the panel to resist loads during handling, transportation, erection, and in-service conditions.

The process used to obtain a thermal or flame finish on granite veneers reduces the effective thickness by about 1/8 in. (3 mm) and the physical strength to a measurable degree [3]. Bushhammered and other similar surface finishes also reduce the effective thickness. For 1 1/4-in. (3-cm)-thick veneers, a reduction in thickness of 1/8 in. (3 mm) reduces the theoretical bending strength by about 20% and increases the elastic deflection under wind loads by about 37%. Laboratory tests on 1 1/4-in. (3-cm)-thick specimens of unaged thermally finished granite revealed that the effects of the thermal finish reduced the bending strength of the specimens by as much as 25 to 30% [4]. The loss of strength depends mainly on the physical properties of the stone-forming minerals, on the coherence of the stone, and on the presence of micro- and macrofractures in the stone.

Thermally finished granite surfaces cause microfracturing, particularly of quartz and feldspars. These microcracks permit absorption of water to a depth of about 1/4 in. (6 mm) in the distressed surface region of the stone, which can result in degradation by cyclic freezing and a further reduction in bending strength.

Weathering is both a chemical decomposition and physical disintegration of stone, and the thinner the stone is sliced, the more susceptible it is to weathering. Simply put, it is possible to diminish the interlocking features of coarse-grained rocks by slicing the minerals too thin.

All natural stones lose strength as a result of aging [thermal cycling, for example, heating to 150°F (66°C) and cooling to −10°F (−23°C), and wet/dry cycling]. The modulus of rupture of building stone can also be affected by freezing and thawing of the stone. Modulus of rupture tests should be conducted on the selected stone at the thickness and surface finish to be used in both the new condition and the condition after 50 cycles of laboratory freeze/thaw testing to determine the reduction in strength, if any. [Suggested freeze-thaw test procedures include: (1) dry cycling between 170°F (77°C) and −10°F (−23°C); and (2) freezing in water at −10°F (−23°C) and thawing in water at room temperature.] Also, stones with a high absorption rate should also be tested in a saturated condition as their flexural, shear, and tensile properties may be significantly lower when wet. Accelerated cyclic temperature tests should also be conducted on the stone-concrete assembly to determine the effect of strength loss on the shear and tensile strengths of the anchors.

For most types of stone, temperature-induced movements are theoretically reversible. However, certain stones, particularly uniform-textured, fine-grained, relatively pure marble, when subjected to a large number of thermal cycles, develop an irreversible expansion in the material amounting to as much as 20% of the total original thermal expansion. This residual growth is caused by slipping of individual calcite crystals with respect to each other [5–7]. Such growth, if not considered in the stone size, design of the anchors, or the stone veneer joints, may result in curling or bowing of thin marble. For relatively thick marble veneers, the expansion effects are restrained or accommodated by the unaffected portion of the veneer. Tests should be performed to establish the minimum thickness required to obtain satisfactory serviceability.

Volume changes due to moisture changes in most stones are relatively small and not a critical item in design, except that bowing of the stone can occur. Moisture permeability of stone veneers is generally not a problem (Table 1) [5]. However, as stone veneers become thinner, water may penetrate in greater amounts and at faster rates than normally expected, and damp-appearing areas of moisture on the exterior surface of thin stone veneers will frequently occur. These damp areas result when the rate of evaporation of water from the stone surface is slower than the rate at which the water moves to the surface.

TABLE 1—*Permeability of commercial building stones,* [5] *in³/h/1/2 in. thickness.*

Stone Type	Pressure, psi		
	1.2	50	100
Granite	0.06 to 0.08	0.11	0.28
Limestone	0.36 to 2.24	4.2 to 44.80	0.9 to 109
Marble	0.06 to 0.35	1.3 to 16.8	0.9 to 28.0
Sandstone	4.2 to 174.0	51.2	221
Slate	0.006 to 0.008	0.08 to 0.11	0.11

NOTE: in³/h/1/2 in. = 16.39 m/h/13 mm.

Stone Sizes

Stone veneers used for precast facing are usually thinner than those used for conventionally set stone with the maximum size generally determined by strength of stone (stone breakage). Thicknesses of marble veneer used on precast concrete have been 7/8 in. (2.2 cm), 1 in. (2.5 cm), 1 1/4 in. (3 cm), 1 1/2 in. (4 cm), and 2 in. (5 cm). Thicknesses of 7/8 in. (2.2 cm) or less are not desirable as it is probable that the anchor will be reflected on the surface and the development of adequate anchor capacity is questionable. Lengths of marble pieces are typically 3 to 5 ft (0.9 to 1.5 m) and widths are 2 to 5 ft (0.6 to 1.5 m) with a maximum area of 20 ft² (1.9 m²) [2]. Travertine has been used in thicknesses of 3/4 in. (1.9 cm), 1 in. (2.5 cm), 1 1/4 in. (3 cm) and 1 1/2 in. (4 cm) with the surface voids filled front and back on the thinner pieces. Thicknesses of 3/4 and 1 in. (2 and 2.5 cm) have resulted in excessive breakage and are not recommended. Lengths varied between 2 to 5 ft (0.6 to 1.5 m) and widths between 1 to 4 ft (0.3 to 1.2 m) with a maximum area of 16 ft² (1.5 m²) [2].

Granite veneer thicknesses used have been 3/4 in. (2 cm), 7/8 in. (2.2 cm), 1 in. (2.5 cm), 1 1/4 in. (3 cm), 1 5/8 in. (4.1 cm), 2 (5 cm) and 2 1/2 in. (6.35 cm) [2]. Thicknesses greater than 1 1/4 in. (3 cm) are recommended, unless strength of stone determined from testing indicates otherwise. Lengths vary from 3 to 7 ft (0.9 to 2.1 m) and widths between 1 to 5 ft (0.3 to 1.5 m) with a maximum area of 30 ft² (2.8 m²).

Limestone thicknesses used for veneer on precast concrete have typically been 1 1/4 in. (3 cm), 1 1/2 in. (3.8 cm), 1 3/4 in. (4.4 cm), and 2 in. (5 cm), although stones as thick as 5 in. (13 cm) have been used. The performance of veneers of thicknesses less than 1 3/4 in. (4.44 cm) is questionable, and their use is not recommended because of potential permeability and strength problems. Length has varied from 4 to 5 ft (1.2 to 1.5 m) and the width between 2 to 4 ft (0.6 to 1.2 m) with a maximum area of 15 ft² (1.4 m²) [2].

The length and width of veneer materials should be sized to a tolerance of +0 −1/8 in. (+0 −3 mm) since a plus tolerance can present problems on precast panels. This tolerance becomes important when trying to line up the false joints on one panel with the false joints on the panel above or below, particularly when there are a large number of pieces of stone on a panel. Tolerance allowance for out-of-square is ±1/16-in. (±1.6-mm) difference in length of the two diagonal measurements. Flatness tolerances for finished surfaces depend on the type of finish. For example, the granite industry tolerances vary from 3/64 in. (1.2 mm) for a polished surface to 3/16 in. (4.8 mm) for flame (thermal) finish when measured with a 4 ft (1.2 m) straightedge [8]. Thickness variations are less important since concrete will provide a uniform back face, except at corner butt joints. In such cases, the finished edges should be within ±1/16 in. (±1.6 mm) of specified thickness. However, large thickness variations may lead to the stone being encased with concrete and thus being unable to move. The aesthetic problems that have occurred with tolerances have been the variation from a flat surface on an exposed face and stone pieces being out of square.

Anchorage of Stone Facing

The precast concrete industry recommends that there be no concrete bonding between stone veneer and concrete backup in order to minimize bowing, cracking, and staining of the veneer. Mechanical anchors should be used to secure the veneer.

The following methods have been used to prevent bond between the veneer and concrete to allow for independent movement: (1) a liquid bond breaker, of a thickness that allows sufficient shear displacement, applied to the veneer back surface prior to placing the concrete; (2) a one component, clear polyurethane coating or other thin liquid bond breaker; (3) a 6 to 10 mil polyethylene sheet; and (4) a closed cell 1/8 to 1/4-in. (3 to 6-mm) polyethylene foam pad [2]. The use of a compressible bond breaker is preferred in order to have movement capability with uneven stone surfaces, either on individual pieces or between stone pieces on a panel.

Stone veneer is usually supplied by the stone fabricator with holes predrilled in the back surface for the attachment of mechanical anchors according to architectural specifications and drawings. Dry (impact) drilling of anchor holes can cause stresses to develop in granite due to differential thermal conditions. If, for example, the granite contains large crystals or materials such as feldspars that possess cleavage, these stresses can cause microfractures in the immediate region of the drilled hole that can propagate for significant distances along cleavage planes. A diamond-cored drilled hole is the recommended type of hole.

Preformed anchors, either 1/8, 5/32, 3/16, or 1/4 in. (3, 4, 5, or 6 mm) in diameter, fabricated from Type 304 or occasionally Type 302 stainless steel, are supplied by the stone fabricator or, in some cases, by the precast producer depending on the contract document requirements. The number and location of anchors should be determined by shear and tension tests conducted on the anchors embedded in a stone/precast concrete test sample and the anticipated loads, wind and shear, to be applied to the panel. Anchor size and spacing in veneers of questionable strengths or with natural planes of weakness may require special analysis.

Four anchors are usually used per stone piece with a minimum of two recommended. The number of anchors has varied from 1 per 1 1/2 ft² (1 per 0.1 m²) of stone to 1 per 6 ft² (1 per 0.6 m²) with 1 per 2 to 3 ft² (1 per 0.2 to 0.3 m²) being the most common. Anchors should be 6 to 9 in. (152 to 229 mm) from an edge with not over 30 in. (760 mm) between anchors. The shear capacity of the spring clip (hairpin) anchors perpendicular to the anchor legs is greater than when they are parallel (Table 2) and depends on the strength of the stone. A typical marble veneer anchor detail with a toe-in spring clip (hairpin) anchor is shown in Fig. 2 and a typical granite veneer anchor detail is shown in Fig. 3. The toed-out anchor in granite may have as much as 50% more tensile capacity than a toed-in anchor, depending on the stone strength.

Depth of anchor holes should be approximately one-half the thickness of the veneer [minimum depth of 3/4 in. (19 mm)] and is often drilled at an angle of 30 to 45° to the plane of the stone. Holes which are approximately 50% oversize have been used to allow for differential movement between the stone and the concrete; however, in most cases, holes 1/16 to 1/8 in. (2 to 3 mm) larger than the anchor are common, as excessive looseness in hole reduces holding power.

Stainless steel dowels, smooth or threaded, are installed to a depth of two thirds the stone thickness with a maximum depth of 2 in. (5 cm) at 45 to 75° angles to the plane of the stone. The minimum embedment in the concrete backup to develop the required bond length is shown in Fig. 5. Dowel size varies from 3/16 to 5/8 in. (5 to 16 mm) for most stones, except that it varies from 1/4 to 5/8 in. (6 to 16 mm) for soft limestone and sandstone and depends

TABLE 2—*Shear capacity of spring clip (hairpin) anchors in granite from various sources.*[a]

Stone	Shear Parallel to Anchor, lb (kg)	Shear Perpendicular to Anchor, lb (kg)
1	2400 to 2650 (1090 to 1200)	3200 to 3500 (1450 to 1590)
2	1800 (815)	2500 (1135)
3	1500 (680)	1500 (680)
4	2500 (1135)	3400 (1540)
5	2800 (1270)	4000 (1815)
6	3400 (1540)	4200 (1905)
7	1000 (455)	1660 (725)

[a] Safety factor needs to be applied.

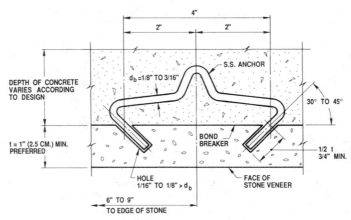

FIG. 2—*Typical anchor for marble veneer.*

on thickness and strength of stone. The dowel hole is usually 1/16 to 1/8 in. (2 to 3 mm) larger in diameter than the anchor (see Figs. 4 and 5).

Limestone has traditionally been bonded and anchored to the concrete because it has the lowest coefficient of expansion. Limestone has also traditionally been used in thicknesses of 3 to 5 in. (8 to 13 cm), but limestone is now being used as thin as 1 1/4 in. (3 cm). When limestone is 2 in. (5 cm) or thinner, it is prudent to use a bond breaker, along with mechanical anchors. Dowels and spring clip anchors have been used to anchor limestone. Typical dowel details for limestone veneers are shown in Figs. 4 and 5. The dowels in Fig. 4 should be inserted at angles alternately up and down to secure stone facing to backup concrete.

It must be emphasized that some flexibility should be introduced with all anchors of stone veneer to precast concrete panels, for example, by keeping the diameter of the anchors to a minimum to allow for the inevitable relative movements which occur with temperature variations and concrete shrinkage. Unaccommodated relative movements can result in excessive stress problems and eventual failure at an anchor location.

There has been a recent trend by some designers to use epoxy to fill the clip anchor or

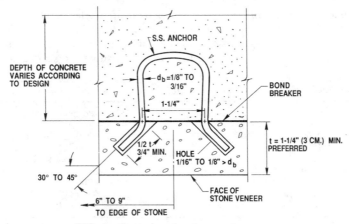

FIG. 3—*Typical anchor for granite veneer.*

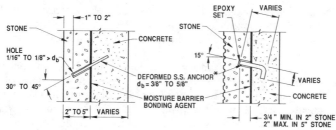

FIG. 4—*Typical anchors for limestone veneer.*

dowel holes in order to eliminate intrusion of water into the holes and the possible dark, damp appearance of moisture on the exposed stone surface. The epoxy increases the shear capacity and rigidity of the anchor. The rigidity may be partially overcome by using 1/2-in. (18-mm)-long compressible rubber or neoprene grommets or sleeves on the anchor at the back surface of the stone. There is also a concern that differential thermal expansion of the stone and epoxy may cause cracking of the stone veneer. However, this may be overcome by keeping the oversizing of the hole to a minimum, thereby reducing epoxy volume. It may be preferable to fill the anchor hole with an elastic fast-curing silicone which has been proven to be nonstaining to light-colored stones, or a low modulus polyurethane sealant. The overall effect of either epoxy or sealant materials on the behavior of the entire veneer should be evaluated prior to their use. At best, the long-term service of epoxy is questionable; therefore, any increase in shear value should not be used in calculating long-term anchor capacity.

When using epoxy in anchor holes, the precaster needs to follow the manufacturer's recommendations as to mixing and curing temperature limitations.

Final design of anchorage and size of the stone should always be based on specific test values for the actual stone to be installed. Anchor test procedures have not been standardized. Test samples for anchor tests should be a typical panel section of about 1 ft² (0.09 m²) and approximate as closely as possible actual panel anchoring conditions. A bond breaker should be placed between stone and concrete during sample manufacture to eliminate any bond between veneer and concrete surface. Each test sample should contain one anchor

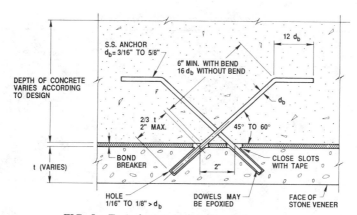

FIG. 5—*Typical cross anchor dowels for stone veneer.*

connecting stone to concrete backup, and a minimum of five tests are needed to determine tensile (pullout) and shear strength of each anchor. Depending on the size of the project, it may be desirable to perform shear and tensile tests of the anchors at intervals during the fabrication period.

The outward wind suction forces on walls parallel to the airstream and on walls at the leeward side of the building are normally the governing design consideration.

Finite-element analysis is a useful technique for evaluating stress in a veneer panel system. This necessitates testing to determine the spring constant values for the material components of the panel in order to model the assembly. Stone veneer should be tested in flexure; the section properties and modulus of elasticity should also be determined. Shear and tensile tests are required for the anchors. The spring constant of a compressible bond breaker should be determined. For insulation, compressive spring constant should be determined and shear spring constant determined, if no bond breaker is used. The 4-in.-diameter concrete plugs encasing the anchors (Fig. 8), when an air space is used, should be treated as a short circular beam. The circular beam and concrete backup can have their properties determined by calculation for use in modelling.

Because of the expected variation in the physical properties of natural stone and the effects of weathering, recommended safety factors are larger than those used for man-made building materials such as steel and concrete. Various safety factors are recommended by the stone trade associations and the suppliers of different kinds of building stones. The minimum recommended design safety factor, based on the average of the test results, is 3 for granite, 4 for anchorage components in granite [8], 8 for limestone veneers [9], and 5 for marble veneers [6]. If the range of test values exceeds the average by more than ±20%, then the safety factor should be applied to the lower bound value. The safety factors in Table 3, based on the coefficient of variation of the test results, have also been recommended for different types of stone [10].

Panel Watertightness

The bond breaker between the stone veneer and concrete backup may function as a vapor barrier on the exterior face of the concrete and tends to keep moisture in the veneer or at the interface unless drainage provisions are provided. Also, after some period of time, gaps may develop between the stone veneer and concrete backup at the bond breaker which could become a location for moisture penetration due to capillary and gravity action, par-

TABLE 3—Safety factors for different types of stone [10].

Type of Stone	Coefficient of Variation	Safety Factor (Based on Average Values)
	IGNEOUS	
	<10	4.5
Granite	10 to 20	6.0
Serpentine	>20	8.0
	METAMORPHIC	
	<10	6.0
Marble	10 to 20	7.5
Slate	>20	10.0
	SEDIMENTARY	
Limestone	<10	7.5
Sandstone	10 to 20	9.0
Travertine	>20	12.0

ticularly where the window or roof design allows water to puddle on top of the panel. One solution that has been used for this problem is a modified rain-screen joint (two-stage joint) as shown in Fig. 6. The approach provides an air-tight 1-in. (25-mm)-wide urethane seal, bonded to the stone veneer and concrete backup and continuous along both sides and top of the panel. Other designers have used a sealant applied to the top and side edges of the stone/concrete interface after the panels are cast. Care must be taken to ensure that the sealant used is compatible with the sealant to be applied to panel joints after erection of the panels.

The bond breaker is not sealed at the bottom of the panel so that any moisture which may get behind the stone veneer can freely drain. In the case of long panels, a sloping gutter is sometimes used, not only under the window, but at every horizontal joint.

Figure 7 shows the construction of an insulated sandwich-veneer precast panel using a logical extension of the modified rain-screen joint. The free movement of the stone veneer is provided by the insulation itself with anchorage of the concrete to the stone similar to Figs. 2 to 5. An air space is not provided and the bottom part of the panel is open at the insulation to drain any possible moisture.

The construction of an insulated sandwich-veneer precast panel with 1/2 to 3/4-in. (13 to 19-mm) air space is shown in Fig. 8. In order to minimize bending of the stone wire anchor, the anchors are embedded in 4-in. (102-mm)-diameter concrete plugs which penetrate the insulation. The plug is separated from the back side of the stone by a small section of a corrugated plastic form liner or voided plastic eggcrate to allow air circulation, or by a polyethylene foam pad. In most cases it has been found that since the concrete plug is separated from the stone, it does not represent a serious thermal bridge, and, to date, major condensation or discoloration of the exterior wall has not been reported.

The air space which is vented via the jointing to the outside environment forms a pressure equalizer. Pressure equalization is achieved by leaving an open horizontal joint at the windows, which necessitates proper flashing details, and by using shiplapped horizontal panel joints which are also left open. With pressure equilization, water should not penetrate the wall system far enough to cause any problems.

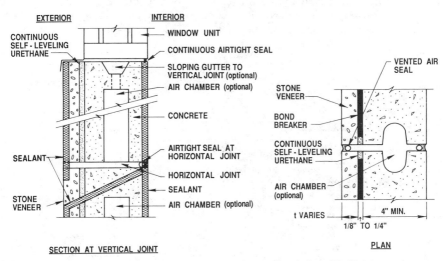

FIG. 6—*Stone veneer precast concrete panel with "modified" joint.*

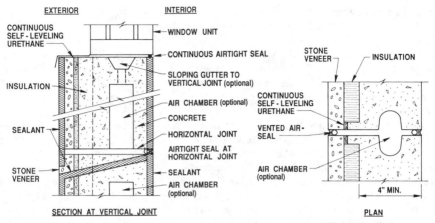

FIG. 7—*Insulated sandwich-veneer precast concrete panel with modified joint.*

Veneer Jointing

Each piece of stone should be positioned and held within established tolerances during fabrication of the panel. Joints between veneer pieces on a precast panel are typically a minimum of 1/4 in. (6 mm), although they have been specified equal to the joint width between precast elements, usually 1/2, 3/4, or 1 in. (13, 19, or 25 mm), depending on the panel size. As actual joint width between precast panels, as erected, depends largely on the accuracy of the main supporting structure, it is not realistic to require matching joint widths between stone pieces and between panels.

Often, an invisible joint is specified, for example, less than 3/16 in. (5 mm), especially on polished veneer. This is simply not possible because the joint must have the width necessary to allow for movements, tolerances, etc. Also, due to tolerances and natural warping, adjacent panels may not be completely flush at the joint and shadow lines will appear. Rather than attempting to hide the joint, the joint should be emphasized by finding an aesthetically pleasing joint pattern with a complementary joint size.

In the form, the veneer pieces are temporarily spaced with a nonstaining, compressible

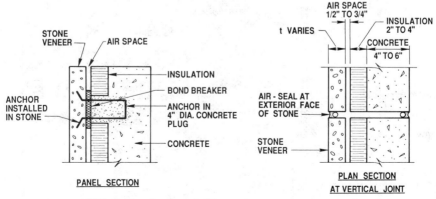

FIG. 8—*Insulated sandwich-veneer precast concrete panel.*

spacing material, such as rubber, neoprene, or soft plastic wedges, or a chemically neutral, resilient, nonremovable gasket, such as sealant backer rod, which will not stain the veneer or adversely affect the sealant to be applied later. Shore A hardness of the gasket should be less than 20. The gaskets should be of a size and configuration that will provide a pocket to receive the sealant and also prevent any of the concrete backup from entering the joints between the veneer units. Nonacidic-based masking or duct tape has also been used to keep concrete out of the stone joints so as to avoid limiting stone movement. Spacer materials should be removed after the panel has been removed from the form unless it is a resilient sealant backup.

Caulking between stones or panels should be an elastomeric—usually urethane, polysulfide, or silicone—that will not stain the stone veneer material. Some grades of silicone sealants are not recommended by their manufacturers for application on high-calcite content materials (marbles) as they may stain light-colored stones. In some projects, caulking between stone pieces on a panel may be installed more economically and satisfactorily at the same time as the caulking between precast elements, while on other projects consideration may be given to caulking the veneer material at the plant. Plant caulking of stone-to-stone joints is recommended in areas subject to freezing and thawing if panels will be left in prolonged storage during winter months.

Handling, Storage, and Shipping

In all operations after removal from forms, veneered precast panels are handled, stored, and shipped on the concrete edge of the panel or on their backs with the stone facing up. The panels must not at any time rest on the veneer face or on any of the veneer edges or corners. To minimize the effects of the sun on bowing, panels are sometimes stored on edge with the length oriented north and south. In order to prevent staining, wood blocking should be covered with a plastic film or some other nonstaining material to prevent contact with the stone veneer. Also, contact between the stone and oil and asphalt-based compounds should be avoided. Once the panels are ready for loading, they may be cleaned (if part of the contractural obligations) with stiff fiber, stainless steel, or bronze wire brushes, a mild soap powder or detergent, and clean water using high pressure, if necessary [11]. No acid or other strong chemicals that might damage or stain the veneer are to be used. Information from stone suppliers on methods of cleaning oil, rust, and dirt stains on stones should be made available to the precast panel producer.

During shipping, the panels may be placed on special rubber-padded racks and care taken to prevent chipping of edges and damage to returns. Long returns at sills and soffits generally create handling problems unless procedures are worked out ahead of time.

Should minor damage occur to the veneer stone during shipping, handling, or erection, field remedial work can successfully be accomplished. Such repairs are normally done by the precaster with repair procedures developed in consultation with the stone fabricator.

Epoxy, stone dust, and a coloring agent, if necessary, are used to repair small chips or spalls. These patches can be finished to the same surface texture as the stone facing. If it is necessary to replace a stone piece, satisfactory techniques have been developed for when the back of the panel is accessible or after the panel has been erected and the back of the panel is inaccessible.

Summary

Stone veneer-faced precast concrete panels have performed with generally excellent results over the past 25 years. They are an economically viable solution to cladding today's structures.

The objectives of both the precaster and the stone fabricator are the same: to provide the owner with the best possible work based on specifications as written. Time and qualified personnel to coordinate the scheduling and delivery must be built into the cost of the job.

References

[1] "PCI Design Handbook, Precast and Prestressed Concrete," 3rd ed., Prestressed Concrete Institute, Chicago, IL, 1985.

[2] Questionnaire on Veneered Faced Panels, Prestressed Concrete Institute, Chicago, IL, August 1986.

[3] "Italian Marble Technical Guide," Volume 1, 1982 ed., Italian Institute for Foreign Trade.

[4] "Design of Thin Stone Veneers on Buildings," I. R. Chin, J. P. Stecich, and B. Erlin, *Building Stone Magazine,* May/June 1986, pp. 50–62.

[5] "Building Construction Handbook," 1st ed., F. S. Merritt, Ed., McGraw-Hill Book Co., Inc., New York, 1958.

[6] "Marble Design Manual," Marble Institute of America, Inc., Farmington, MI, 1976.

[7] "Marble Engineering Handbook," Marble Institute of America, Inc., Farmington, MI, 1962.

[8] "Specifications for Architectural Granite, 1986 Edition," National Building Granite Quarries Association, Inc., West Chelmsford, MA.

[9] "Indiana Limestone Handbook, 1984–1985," Indiana Limestone Institute of America, Inc., Bedford, IN.

[10] "Design Considerations for Using Stone Veneer on High-Rise Buildings," Gere, A. S., this publication.

[11] *Cleaning Stone and Masonry, ASTM STP 935,* J. R. Clifton, Ed., American Society for Testing and Materials, Philadelphia, 1986.

Bibliography

"Marble-Faced Precast Panels," National Association of Marble Producers, 1966.

"Marble-Faced Precast Panels," McDaniel, W. B., *PCI Journal,* Vol. 12, No. 4, Aug. 1967, pp. 29–37.

Grant Kafarowski[1]

Stone on Precast Concrete or Steel in Wall Design and Construction

REFERENCE: Kafarowski, G., **"Stone on Precast Concrete or Steel in Wall Design and Construction,"** *New Stone Technology, Design, and Construction for Exterior Wall Systems, ASTM STP 966,* B. Donaldson, Ed., American Society for Testing and Materials, Philadelphia, 1988, pp. 105–118.

ABSTRACT: After a brief discussion of building stone geology and quarrying, and the cutting/finishing operations, the paper discusses various aspects of the quality control and tolerances of panel construction as they affect the fabricator and erector and ultimately the finished stone panel system.

KEY WORDS: precast concrete, wall design, stone panels, wall systems

A building is many things to many people. To those of us involved with its design or construction it represents a more or less successful accomplishment of our ideas. To a stone panel fabricator it gives the satisfaction of having completed a complex production cycle involving many men and skills, who in the process transform a stone into a component of a sophisticated wall system that creates a controlled environment.

Each of the thousands of stones of a building is exposed to a human decision and contact—hence potential error and damage—during any of the 23 independent manufacturing and erection operations that are necessary to get the stone from a distant quarry to the building. Each operation involves people with a specific skill who, day by day with an average effort, produce a range of quality that is determined by the project requirements.

The designer, by evaluating the project requirements in the context of such limitations, will not only obtain an optimum quality but will also ultimately enhance the performance of the building.

Geology

Natural stone is a rock comprising an assemblage of minerals and is one of three broad geological groups: (1) igneous; (2) sedimentary; and (3) metamorphic.

1. *Igneous Rocks*

These originated below the Earth's surface and solidified from a hot molten condition, for example, granite, basalt, etc. The texture (the relative size and arrangement of component minerals) is determined by the rock mode of formation. When cooled slowly, it is entirely crystalline and even grained. With rapid cooling at or near the Earth's surface it may be entirely vitreous or fine grained with some large crystals. During crystallization,

---

[1] Artex, P.O. Box 149, LAK 1B2, Concord, Ontario, Canada.

different constituents combine to form crystals of silicate minerals, and any excess silica forms quartz.

Granite—In terms of mineral composition this rock contains 20 to 40% quartz, 50% light (orthoclase) and/or dark (plagioclase) feldspar, and 5 to 10% mica. It is an excellent structural stone because of its high strength, hardness, and resistance to weathering.

2. *Sedimentary Rocks*

These form a thin layer of the Earth's surface covering the older igneous and metamorphic rocks. They are made of fragments and particles derived from older rocks that disintegrated and weathered at the Earth's surface; after being subjected to the process of cementation, compaction, and hardening, they have become a firm and coherent mass of new rock, for example, limestone, travertine, and dolomite.

The carbon and sulfur dioxide in the atmosphere, combined with rain water, form weak-acid solutions which slowly dissolve the surface layers of these rocks.

Limestone—This rock is a small part of this group and is formed by either chemical deposition or from organic remains. It consists essentially of calcium and magnesium carbonate with minute amounts of quartz and is usually white or gray in color, although a tint may be produced by various mineral impurities.

Dolomite—This rock is a result of a replacement process known as a metasomatism whereby the original minerals of the limestone are changed atom by atom into new minerals by the agency of percolating solutions.

Travertine—This rock is made of chemically deposited calcium carbonate from saturated solutions near a calcareous spring. Its characteristic cellular structure is because it's a coating to vegetable matter.

3. *Metamorphic Rocks*

These are both igneous and sedimentary rocks exposed to new conditions of heat and pressure, for example, marble, slate. New minerals grow in the solid with the help of small amounts of solvents, so that resulting textures are entirely different from the original rocks. The size of crystals is increased with the prolonged action of heat.

Marble—This rock is a metamorphic product of limestone—essentially calcium carbonate—colored by traces of the original rock deposits.

Faults

Under action of the Earth's movements the rock may change its relative position with or without resulting cracks, which may or may not be filled by inclusions of molten rocks, thus forming veins.

Stone Manufacture

1. *Quarrying*

The stone is quarried by blasting and/or splitting along a series of ±1½ in. dia holes about 12 in. on centers defining the block required. The size is preferably 5 by 5 by 10 ft or 48 000 lb, as this is a generally accepted shipping weight.[2]

[2] 1 in. = 2.54 cm; 1 lb = 0.45 kg; 1 ft. = 0.30 m.

Faults—The pressure under which the block was formed is relieved when the block is taken out of the surrounding mass of rock, and relief of that pressure results in fine micro-cracks on its surface. These cracks are smaller if the blocks are allowed to cure over a long period of time.

2. *Cutting*

The blocks are cut using gang saws, the blades of which are spaced to the required thickness of the slab required, and the whole block is sliced vertically down in one operation through reciprocal movement of the blades, which slide on an abrasive slurry.

Faults—In handling bundles of slabs using belts or cable wrapped around them, the outer slabs may be damaged in shifting against each other, especially if the edges of the slabs contain innate cracks from the block itself. As the saw wears out, the iron particles become embedded in the cut surface and will rust unless washed off. In polishing, this rust is removed from the surface; in honing or flaming some rust may remain and in extreme cases may become objectionable.

Tolerance—Assuming no error in presetting the blades, the resulting thickness will vary depending on the tension and wear condition of the blade, the quality of abrasive slurry, and the local hardness within the block itself, especially with a hard material such as granite. The result is normally $\pm \frac{3}{16}$ in. within a 2 to 3 ft length of finished stone, although $\pm \frac{1}{4}$ to $\frac{5}{16}$ in. is possible. The sliced block is then separated into smaller bundles and delivered to surface-finishing machines for honing, polishing, or flaming.

3. *Surface Finishing*

The individual slabs travel on horizontal conveyors, and a top-mounted rotary grinder traverses the slab and produces the finished surface required, which is determined by different grit sizes.

Honing (*Grit 240 to 300*)—This is the first stage of the polishing operation, leveling the surface but hiding the true color of the stone as the roughness creates an overall gray hue. There is a major difference in color between the dry (gray) and wet (dark true color) stone.

Polishing (*Grit 800 to 1200*)—This is accomplished by using a progressively finer stone and grinding powder. The polishing brings out the natural color of the material and effectively seals the surface, thus making it less permeable to moisture compared to other surface finishes.

Faults—With the slab wet, all faults of the surface such as inclusions and cracks are noticeable.

Tolerance—Since the thickness and local hardness varies, the finished surface is rarely a plane. Also, most machines have floating grinder heads which follow the surface. The normal variation is $+0$, $-\frac{1}{16}$ over a 3 to 4 in. length.

Flaming—Open flame heat is designed to raise the surface temperatures as fast as possible and is followed by immediate cooling that results in a cracking and splitting away of a thin $\frac{1}{16}$ to $\frac{1}{8}$ in. layer of surface material. In one method, a torch with a jet of water traverses the stationary slab. In another, a stationary line of torches followed by a line of water jets is positioned over a moving slab. The result of the process is the true color of individual crystals. All natural inclusions and imperfections are easily visible.

Faults—The principle of the finish is the rapid heating and cooling of the surface layer only. In practice, this is not always possible, with the result being the microcracking of part of the thickness of the slab. This will be more frequent in granite rich in black ferromagnesium minerals. With a single torch configuration, the longitudinal speed of the conveyor must be carefully coordinated with the traverse speed and intensity of the torch or else the resulting panel will have a definite wavy surface.

Tolerance—Out of plane variation +0, −⅛ in 12 in.

4. *Cutting*

For standard square cuts there are at least two methods:

a. *Single slab*—A single slab is cut on continuous conveyors set at right angles to each other with rotary diamond blade saws mounted on traverse beams above.
b. *Multiple slab*—A stack of several slabs is cut to a required width in one direction followed by rotating the stack under the blade to a required angle for the second cut.

Faults—If, as is usual, the finished face of the stone is cut facing the blade, then any chips or breaks are on the back face, which is not seen.

Tolerance—Method a, with the right angle preset into the machine itself, is accurate (±1/16 in.) with a rare ±⅛ in. Method b, where every stone is rotated, relies more on the condition and proper maintenance of the machine, and the ±⅛ in. variation is more frequent.

Special Cuts–Miters

These are made after the standard square cut as a separate operation.

Faults—Since the slabs are stored and handled vertically, the sloping edge is easily damaged, especially if both edges are miters. Sharp edges should be removed by grinding off 3/16 to ¼ in. of the pointed ends.

Tolerance—Any variation of the miter angle is easily absorbed within the joint depth.

5. *Drilling*

Holes above 3/16 in. diameter are drilled using high-speed diamond drills. Impact drill for holes greater than ⅛ in. must be used with caution, especially near or at the edge since they may produce microcracks around the holes. An angle of less than 45° should be avoided because of drilling difficulties (drill slippage and drill bit breakage).

6. *Crating*

There are two basic types:

a. Fully closed boards.
b. Open frame.

Open frame is preferable for ease of opening, access, and waste disposal as well as for inspection on delivery. Care must be taken to protect the granite with polyethylene against wood staining that may occur as a result of exposure to rain, etc. As a rule, limiting 12 to 16 slabs of granite per crate is better, as generally there is less damage and easier access to specials than in a crate containing a larger number of panels.

7. *Shipping*

For boat shipment, the crates with vertical panels and thin spacers between them are loaded in a container. For road shipment the panels are strapped into bundles and loaded on trailers.

Damage—In general, since more time, thought, and effort are put into crating and container loading, there is less damage in transportation. However, because of thickness variation, vibration, and impact, local cracking within a crate may occur.

The percentage of damage is up to 2 to 3% by road and 1 to 2% in container shipment, with the amount varying with the size of panels. Damage of large (5 ft^2 and up) and thin and long (4 in. by 4 ft. and up) panels is more frequent, especially if the sizes are mixed in a crate.

Physical Properties

Strength

Strength varies with:

1. Moisture content—the wet material has lower strength than the dry.
2. Direction of test relative to the grain; parallel to the grain has lower strength than perpendicular.
3. Size of crystals relative to thickness. Where crystal size is close to the thickness, the strength is reduced.
4. Flaming reduces the strength.
5. The strength of long narrow panels is less than the same length of nearly square panels.

Moisture

Veneer stone is relatively permeable, absorbing and transporting moisture by capillary action. This is particularly noticeable near the ground (where the moisture may travel upwards several inches) or near any porous water-holding material in direct contact (for example, open cell backer rod).

Temperature

The veneer stone temperature varies with the ambient air temperature and its rate of change. Thus the night-day temperature of the north elevation will be close to the surrounding air, whereas the west and south exposed to the direct heat of the sun may go up to 160°F. Under these conditions there is a temperature gradient across the thickness of the stone creating a bowing effect. These temperature-induced length and curvature changes, if restrained, will create internal stresses, the effect of which is significant for thin irregular-shaped slabs. (See Fig. 1.)

Load W

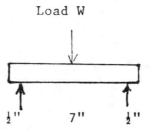

FIG. 1—*Test results. Modulus of rupture of 8 by 4 by 1¼-in. granite.*

Modulus of Rupture = BM/S = W7 by 6/4 by 4 by 125².

Granite Type	Finish	Modulus of Rupture, psi, 1¼-in. Granite
1	Polished	1250
1	Flamed	925
2	Flamed	900
3	Polished	1280
3	Flamed	550[a]

NOTE: When tested according to ASTM on 2-in. granite, the modulus of rupture for Type 1-2000 psi; Type 2-1500 psi; Type 3-2100 psi.

[a] This specimen originally polished was hand flamed in the testing lab.

Architectural Considerations

General

Just as brick buildings are designed around a brick size module, veneer stone should be given the same consideration. Once a conceptual design is prepared, this should be analyzed with a view to establish a typical dimensional module for the stone which should be used throughout—any variation made up with specials. In turn, the specials should be analyzed to combine as many as possible within a minimum number of different types. It is rare that typical units cause problems, but quite often the specials, essential to the continuity of panel production, do not fit or are missing. Normally the larger the number of types containing smaller number of units, the greater is the chance of error.

1. *Appearance.* From a knowledge of its formation one can anticipate the appearance of the finished cut veneer stone. Finely crystalline (¼ in. to ⅜-in. crystals) will generally give a uniform appearance, whereas small crystals interspersed with large may result in a color variation depending on the position of the cut relative to the location of large crystals (see Fig. 2).

Cut 1
Cut 2
Cut 3

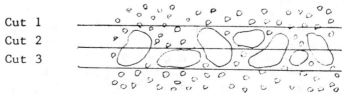

FIG. 2—*Color variation.*

Thickness	Length L FT	
	←——L——→ .2L ↑ .6L↑ .2L	↓ L ↑
3/4"	2.58'	1.16'
1"	4.4'	1.98'
1¼"	6.9'	3.1'

FIG. 3—*Theoretical size of granite for 65 psf wind and 300 psi bending stress.*

With contrasting small and large crystals, Cuts 1 and 3 will look similar and have the color of the small crystals. Cut 2 will have the color of 50% large + 50% small.

2. *Size and thickness.* These are related as shown in Fig. 3 based on a 65 psf wind pressure and a 300 psi bending stress in the panel.

To these values a tolerance of + ⅛ should be added to get an approximate minimum thickness of engineered stone.

3. *Shape.* Rectangular stone with a square cut is a standard. Irregular shapes should be used with great caution as they may result in a system that is prone to breakage during handling or later in place. Large sizes should be typical, small sizes special. To reduce the anchor costs, the sizes should be as large as possible.

4. *Edges.* Where possible, miters should be avoided, especially on triangular shapes where the miters create a sharp point (Fig. 4).

5. *Joints.* These should be ⁵⁄₁₆ in. minimum to allow for tolerance and to ensure that the caulking is a minimum ³⁄₁₆ in. (Note: Caulking manufacturer's minimum joint is ¼ in.)

Design Considerations of Veneer Panels

General

There are two basic concepts:

1. Stone veneer acts as an air barrier and takes the full wind forces and transfers them to the structure. For this to be effective, the joints must be fully and effectively sealed to stop rainwater from being driven into the building, and in pressurized, humidified buildings the insulation attached to the granite must be covered with a continuous vapor barrier on the warm side. The granite and its anchors take all wind forces. The supporting structure must be designed to allow for cyclical thermal variation.

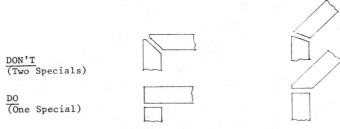

DON'T
(Two Specials)

DO
(One Special)

FIG. 4—*Edge conditions.*

FIGS. 5, 6—*Conventional U-type anchorage pin (left) and preferred version (right).*

2. *Rain screen concept.* The stone acts as a rain barrier only and is supported by an air barrier system. It is essentially a cavity-wall, double-glazing concept, where the inner skin insulated on the outside provides an air-vapor barrier and structural supporting system and is separated by an air space from the outer skin, which protects it from the rain only. The air cavity has to be vented and drained to the outside to eliminate a pressure difference as well as to remove any moisture that may enter it. The continuity of the inner skin and its seal, responsible for separating the inside of the building from the outside, is critical in modern pressurized buildings to stop movement of humidified air in and out of the building with resulting condensation within the insulation. Being protected from the sun and thermal variation, the life of the seal, generally caulking, is extended. Inasmuch as the outside skin seal, normally caulking or gasketing, need not be perfect, the inside seal has to be carefully detailed to allow an easy access for proper workmanship and inspection.

Both systems have their advantages and disadvantages. In the first system the stone with its supporting framing (steel or precast concrete) undergoes a thermal and building movement. Therefore the stone and panel joints have to be carefully detailed to allow for the movement to take place within the elastic properties of the sealant. Also, access has to be provided for proper placing of the insulation and continuous vapor barrier to stop internal condensation.

In the second system, pressure equalization and drainage are sometimes difficult to accomplish. The window design has to be such that the vapor seal between the glass and the granite panel is continuous and unbroken. The access for inside caulking has to be provided. However, controlled plant conditions allow better and easier workmanship with resulting improved quality and time savings.

Anchorages

1. *Conventional anchorages in precast concrete.* These are U-type pins as shown in Fig. 5. The spacing is generally one per 2 to 3 ft². Structurally the pin depends on the bond and bearing capacity of the epoxy to develop a bending moment in the pin which, when its stress reaches the yield point, pulls out.

A preferred version of the above is as shown in Fig. 6. Here the pins develop the bending moment without help from the epoxy. The neoprene tube provides some ductility to the

FIG. 7—*Expansion bolt. Note: this is a proprietary expansion bolt and should not be confused with a typical masonry expansion bolt.*

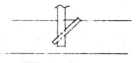

FIG. 8—*Crosspin.*

connection, thus providing for the thermal movement of the granite. In arranging the anchoring pins, consideration should be given to the deflected convex or concave shape of the granite. Therefore the pins should be kept away from the center of the granite. The diameter of the pin is sized to resist the wind forces and thermal cycling of the granite without reaching yield point.

The above is a useful anchorage system for granites whose structural properties are uncertain.

2. *Engineereed anchorages.* These are based on four-point anchor systems, two of which carry the gravity loading (including 100% impact). All four carry the wind forces. They would generally be arranged at the fifth points of the panel so as to minimize the stress in the granite. Arranging gravity fixings near the top is preferred by the author, as this makes the job site replacement operation easier and safer.

Examples of mechanical anchorages are seen in Figs. 7 and 8. Both can be used with either steel or concrete systems (see Fig. 9).

3. *Joint sealing.* This is usually caulking, whose elongation should be limited to not more than 20%. For two-part material, a thorough 3 to 5 min mixing with a properly designed paddle is critical. By making the supporting structure joint ⅛ in. greater than the granite joint, the risk of damage during handling is greatly reduced.

Correct venting of rain screen panels is essential to allow for an efficient air circulation.

Granite Type	Anchor Type	Pin Diameter	Pull - Out Load lb	
			With Epoxy	Without Epoxy
2	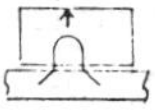	3/16"	700	300
2	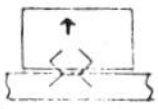	⅛"	–	550
3	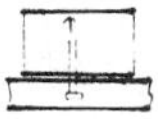	3/16" Exp. Bolt*	–	1300
3	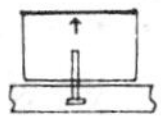	3/8" Exp. Bolt*	–	1900
1	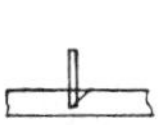	5/16" Cross Pin	2600	2100
1	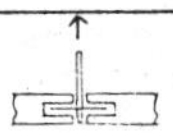	3/16" Edge Dowel	–	900

FIG. 9—*Anchors pullout tests on 6 by 6 by 1¼-in. granite. *This is a proprietary expansion bolt and should not be confused with a typical masonry expansion bolt.*

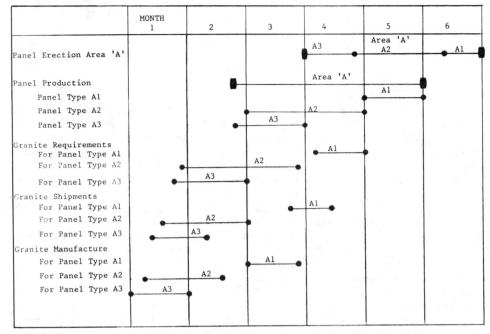

FIG. 10—*Example of planning schedule.*

Planning

Because of the extended time lag between quarrying and delivery to the panel fabricator's yard, this is one of the most important elements of successful plant production of granite-faced panels. It becomes critical where a large number of different types, shapes, and sizes are a characteristic of the job. In this situation it is normal to manufacture all standard stones, high volume sizes first, leaving the specials till last. To avoid delays, recriminations, etc., it is essential to plan an erection sequence, fit production within its limitations, and then schedule the individual granite slabs to match the panel production. Unless this is done, either the panel production comes to a stop or panels are made leaving out a space for the job site application later.

If possible, detailing individual crating requirements eliminates extensive multiple handling of each granite slab within the crate and the accumulation of partly open crates occupying valuable production space. A schedule (Fig. 10) of that depth constantly monitored will eliminate 90% of problems. To allow for the remainder, a constant stock of the five to six largest sizes of granite, which can be cut as required to fill in the missing or damaged stones, is absolutely essential.

Manufacture and Erection of Granite-Faced Precast Panels

1. *Unloading.* At the time of unloading the crates from a container (open top preferable) or trailers, the condition of the load and crates, as well as—in the case of open crates—superficial-edge damage and thickness of the granite, can be inspected. The requirement of a specification to "inspect and accept within two weeks" or similar would mean uncrating and crating back all granite. This is cost prohibitive and impractical.

2. *Storing.* Crates of granite are stored on a sound, level, dry, and well-drained surface away from contaminants, moving equipment, etc. They should not be stockpiled on top of each other because of access problems, possible damage, etc.

3. *Placing granite in a panel form.* At this point slabs are transferred from a vertical to a horizontal position. Panels up to 150 to 180 lb can be manhandled; above that weight a crane is required with scissors or similar attachment, allowing an easy withdrawal after granite is laid down. The granite is placed on 6 by 3 by 1-in. neoprene pads located at each corner, thus allowing proper alignment with the adjoining slabs. For large slabs—over 5 ft—additional soft pads at midpoint may be required to reduce the danger of accidental overstress. Every second joint is correctly spaced to a reference point marked on the form, thus taking out the size variation and reducing the possibility of misalignment. Once spaced out, the joints are blocked with small polyethylene pads to prevent movement of the panels during subsequent operations.

4. *Anchors.* Prior to placing the anchors (A304 stainless steel), the hole should be air blown and dry to receive epoxy.

5. *Uninsulated panels.* A bond breaker—⅛ in. close-cell polyethylene sheeting—prevents the back face irregularities of the granite from being locked in the concrete and allows for in/out thermal deflection. It also makes replacement of the granite slab easier, allowing some thickness tolerance. The bond breaker should be sealed around the anchors and panel perimeter to stop the concrete from touching the granite.

6. *Insulated panels.* The insulation, usually Styrofoam SM, is placed on spacers with the joints glued and made tight at the anchors and panel perimeter.

7. *Reinforcing.* In placing a prefabricated reinforcing cage, care must be taken to ensure that the anchors are not disturbed and, with the cage in final position, that they are not touching the reinforcing cage. Unless the stainless steel is passivated, an electrochemical reaction between the two steels may occur in the presence of moisture.

8. *Concrete.* Concrete has to be carefully and uniformly distributed over the entire panel to avoid local overload. It is then vibrated, troweled, and allowed to cure.

9. *Lifting from the form.* The location of the crane lifting points has to be carefully designed to ensure that at no time will the granite touch the form, as generally this will crack the granite. A tilting table is far safer in this respect and should be used whenever possible.

10. *Storing.* The panels are stored in a vertical position on bearing points away from the granite. This is sometimes difficult and therefore expensive to accomplish on spandrel panels having a granite soffit.

11. *Shipping.* Panels are shipped on trailers specially fitted to carry the granite panel in such a way that at all times the granite is not in contact with any supports, bracing, etc., as this will cause damage. The shipping method has to be coordinated with the erection to ensure easy and damage-free lifting from the trailer as this is the most damage-prone operation.

12. *Hoisting.* Once the panel is lifted off the trailer and brought to the correct height and location, approaching the building face is the next damage-prone instance, as a slight misjudgement on the part of the floor crew and the crane operator will result in damage to the panel itself and its neighbors. To a lesser extent, accidents may occur at the final stage of lowering the panel onto its bearings, where similar damage may occur.

13. *Alignment.* Because of the rigidity of the concrete panel, this is normally trouble free. It is done in three stages.

a. Each bearing end of the panel is brought to its correct height.

b. Each end fixing is brought to the correct location from the building face both horizontally and vertically.

c. Because of the panel stiffness, the intermediate connections need little or no adjustment.

Manufacture and Erection of Granite-Faced Steel Insulated Panels

1. *Placing granite in a panel form.* The procedure is similar to precast concrete.
2. *Drilling of holes.* Because of the variation in granite sizes, the holes are drilled after the granite is laid and joints spaced out in the panel form. The holes are drilled to a template which matches the holes in the steel frame.
3. *Anchors.* They are located as for precast concrete.
4. *Insulation.* Fiberglass insulation with pins attached is placed on spacers laid on the granite. Glue is then spread over the insulation and pins.
5. *Steel frame.* Steel frame, prefabricated on a separate jig with galvanized sheet metal welded to it, is laid on top of the insulation and pressed into it to correct depth. The anchorage of the granite to the steel is then completed and a stainless steel flashing is laid in a caulking bead bolted to the steel; the back of the steel panel is then painted.
6. *Lifting from the form.* As for precast concrete.
7. *Storing.* As for precast concrete.
8. *Shipping.* As for precast concrete except that, because of panel flexibility, additional intermediate tiebacks are required.
9. *Hoisting.* Similar to precast, other than additional pickup points are required to stabilize the compression flange of the panel.
10. *Alignment.* This has to take into account the flexibility of the panel, and a systematic procedure must be designed so that the panel is never exposed to undue twisting, which might overstress the granite.

Comparison of Precast Concrete and Steel Granite-Faced Panels

1. *Design.* The design of steel panel is much more detailed and has to take into account many more factors than precast concrete.
2. *Manufacture.* Many matching precision jigs are required for successful production of steel panels. The training of personnel is more extensive, and the tolerances are much tighter than for precast concrete.
3. *Erection.* Because of its flexibility, the erection procedures of steel panels are different from rigid concrete panels and are more difficult to understand and accept by the erection personnel.
4. *Costs.* On a small project, set up, engineering, and training costs for steel panels are high. On large projects they become insignificant and overall savings make them economical.

Building "B", Battery Park, New York

This project is of interest for its unique problems created by material and jointing change.

It was originally designed as a 12 ft, 9 in. by 30 ft granite-faced insulated precast concrete window panel with panel joints at floor line, with windows integral with a liner and extending in and forming a trim to the finished Sheetrock (Fig. 11). For various reasons, this was later changed to a granite-insulated steel panel with the horizontal panel joints moved down to the top of the window line. To drain the air cavity, a continuous flashing was provided at

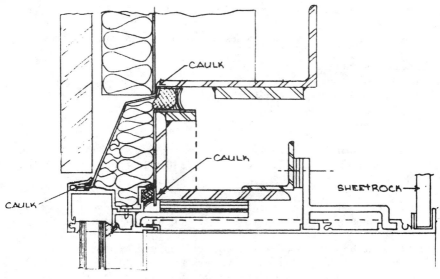

HEAD DETAIL

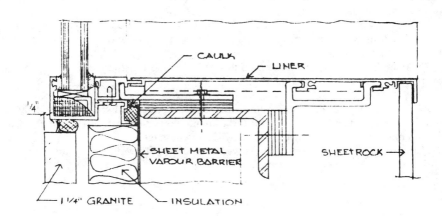

SILL DETAIL

FIG. 11—*Battery Park window detail.*

the bottom of each panel (above the head of window), and this engaged into a window head flashing, thus providing a positive drainage of the cavity.

These changes effectively eliminated any vertical manufacturing and erection tolerance of the panel. Furthermore, since the window with its integral liner had to relate to both outside line of granite and inside line of Sheetrock with three windows in a 30-ft panel, it not only meant that the overall panel thickness had to be controlled very closely, but also that the overall panel had to be manufactured and erected with a minimum deviation from a plane.

Based on this analysis, the production design had to accommodate the following:

1. Front face of granite -0, $+\frac{1}{8}$.
2. Inside face of granite to sheet metal $-\frac{1}{8}$, $+\frac{3}{16}$.
3. Steel framing shape variation -0, $+\frac{1}{8}$.
4. 30 ft by 12 ft, 9 in. steel welding distortion -0, $+\frac{3}{16}$.
5. Erection tolerance in 30 ft, $\pm\frac{3}{16}$.

To manufacture at the schedule requirement of up to six 12 ft, 9 in. by 30 ft panels of this precision per day, the panel was divided into three 10 by 12 ft modules, made on separate jigs as follows:

1. Steel angles and plates were saw-cut on jigs with built-in variable stops to $-\frac{1}{16}$ tolerance.
2. Press punching up to ten holes for granite anchors was done simultaneously on preset jigs.
3. 10 ft by 12 ft, 9 in. steel module was assembled on a jig, holding individual members in their designated position, maintaining the sides and top, allowing any tolerance to accumulate in the bottom, and corrected for welding distortion by differential camber.
4. Rigid steel tray for placing the granite with window dimensions fixed, top and bottom held, tolerance in the side and bottom joints.
5. Drilling of holes after granite was placed and correctly spaced to a jig, matching holes in steel members.
6. A matching station where the steel module was placed on the rigid tray and correctly located at four corner points with reference to the plane of and the granite itself and steel bolted in the granite.
7. Assembly table where three modules were welded together to form a 30 ft by 12 ft, 9 in. panel.

After manufacture the panels were caulked, stockpiled, and shipped vertically on frame trailers. Provision of long dowels on the trailers allowed control of the panel during crane pickup and prevented an uncontrolled swing and damage.

Using this sytem, over 1000 panels were manufactured well within the tolerances listed above and the schedule requirements.

Hugh F. Kluesner, Jr.[1]

Posttensioned Panels of Indiana Limestone

REFERENCE: Kluesner, H. F. Jr., **"Posttensioned Panels of Indiana Limestone,"** *New Stone Technology, Design, and Construction for Exterior Wall Systems, ASTM STP 996*, B. Donaldson, Ed., American Society for Testing and Materials, Philadelphia, 1988, pp. 119–127.

ABSTRACT: Posttensioning of concrete for various uses has been standard practice in the construction industry for many years. The engineering principles are well-known. The design of tensioned stone panels utilizes these same principles, and the advantages of posttensioned stone are much the same as for concrete. Most applications to date have been for cladding only. This paper is essentially a summary of experiences on projects utilizing posttensioned units of Indiana limestone for which the author developed the posttensioned designs and plant procedures. It is not intended to be a design manual but to provide a few guidelines for use in adapting well-known posttensioning methods to the design of natural stone units. This paper includes information on design loads, tendon design, allowable stresses, epoxy joints between stones, gravity and retention connections, grouting, fabrication, handling, storage, and transport considerations. It also includes case histories of projects.

KEY WORDS: posttension, limestone, cladding

Background

Posttensioning of concrete for various uses has been standard practice in the construction industry for many years. The engineering principles are well-known. The design of tensioned stone panels utilizes these same principles with some variations as required by the characteristics of the stone to be used and the application details.

Early experiments with posttensioned Indiana limestone units were sponsored by the Building Stone Institute in 1967 and by the Indiana Limestone Institute in 1970. In these programs, several posttensioned beams and slabs were fabricated and tested. The results of both programs clearly indicated the potential for this procedure in the cladding of buildings with stone.

The advantages of posttensioned stone are much the same as for concrete. It permits the stone to carry larger loads over longer spans than would be possible with conventional units. The stone units can be plant-fabricated in much larger units to span column to column in the building. Window systems can be carried directly on the stone panels, thereby eliminating a separate window support system. The panels are constructed entirely of stone, requiring no steel truss or other secondary framing to carry design loads. Transportation breakage is virtually nonexistent because tensile bending stresses are low or eliminated entirely by the tensioning procedure. Square-foot erection costs are reasonable since each lift represents a large panel area.

Most applications to date have been for cladding only. A few structural applications have been built using beams for such building features as porticoes, where the live loads have been limited to roof loads and wind loads.

[1] President, Kluesner Engineering, Inc., Bedford, IN 47421.

This paper is essentially a summary of experiences on projects utilizing posttensioned units of Indiana limestone for which the author developed the posttensioned designs and plant procedures. This is not intended to be a design manual. It is intended to provide a few guidelines for use in adapting well-known posttensioning methods to the design of natural stone units.

Design Guidelines

The following are design considerations which must be addressed:

1. Determine Design Loads
   a. Calculate vertical loads on the panel due to panel weight plus weight of walls or windows above.
   b. Calculate horizontal loads due to positive and negative wind perpendicular to the panel face.
   c. Calculate horizontal loads due to seismic action, if applicable. Seismic loads may occur horizontally from any direction. Most codes do not require that wind and seismic loads occur simultaneously for design purposes. The maximum horizontal design load perpendicular to the face of the panel may be either due to wind or seismic, depending upon the wind and seismic geographical zones involved. Maximum horizontal design loads parallel to the wall are almost always due to seismic forces.
2. Tendon Design
   Determine tendon tension and location required to limit stone-bending stresses to allowable values.
   a. The maximum allowable stone tensile stress due to bending should be limited to a maximum of one-eighth the modulus of rupture. For best design, tensile stress can be limited to zero in most applications. Maximum allowable compressive stress should be limited to one-eighth the compressive strength of the stone. In almost all cases, the tensile stress will govern.
   b. The initial tendon tension (at lock off) should be calculated to allow for 15% long-term tension losses due to steel relaxation and stone creep. This value is commonly used for concrete design and is a conservative figure for Indiana limestone since shrinkage of the stone does not occur. The location of the tendon (or tendons) is a function of the member's section properties and the design requirements. The centerline of the tendon is always located relative to the section centroid. In other cases, it is necessary to place it below the centroid in order to develop a moment in the member to resist the vertical loads and to keep bottom fiber tensile stresses within allowable values. Sometimes the tendon location is dictated by edge distance (distance from centerline tendon to edge of stone) due to shear stresses under the tendon anchor plate. Figure 1 illustrates the traditional engineering formulae to determine tendon force. Once this force has been calculated, the proper tendon size can be selected from the tendon manufacturer's technical data.
   c. Many types of tendons are available. The author favors the DYWIDAG[2] threadbar system. This system is a threaded rod which utilizes a nut on each end to provide a positive lock to maintain the rod tension.

[2] DYWIDAG threadbar Posttensioning system, Dyckerhoff & Widmann, Inc., Lemont, IL.

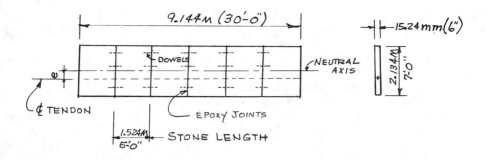

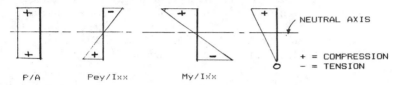

STRESS @ CENTERLINE PANEL DUE TO GRAVITY LOADS ONLY

DESIGNED FOR "O" TENSION IN BOTTOM FIBER

$P/A + Pey/I_{xx} - My/I_{xx} = 0$ (BOTTOM FIBER)

P/A = COMPRESSIVE STRESS DUE TO TENDON TENSION

Pey/I_{xx} = FIBER STRESS (BENDING) DUE TO TENDON ECCENTRICITY (e)

My/I_{xx} = FIBER STRESS (BENDING) DUE TO GRAVITY LOADS

SOLVE FOR P (FINAL TENDON TENSION)

P_1 = INITIAL (LOCK OFF) TENDON TENSION

$P_i = P/.85$ FOR 15% LOSSES

FIG. 1—*Traditional engineering formulae to determine tendon force.*

3. Allowable Stresses
   a. All stone stresses should be limited to the values listed in "Technote on Safety Factors" (Indiana Limestone Institute of America, Bedford, Indiana).
   b. Tendon stresses should be limited to values as recommended by the tendon manufacturer.
   c. Steel hardware stresses should be in accordance with the American Institute of Steel Construction, Chicago.
4. Tendon Anchor Plate
   a. The plate size must be designed to limit stone compression and shear to allowable values.
   b. Plate thickness must be sufficient to limit plate-bending stress to proper values.
   c. The plate must be attached to the stone with a full bed of epoxy between plate and stone. The epoxy must be cured to a hard state prior to tensioning the tendon.

This is necessary to provide a uniform distribution of the tendon force over the stone area; otherwise "high spots" may develop stone stress concentrations and potential spalling of the stone.

    d. The plate must be provided with a bleedhole to allow air to escape as grout is pumped into the hole to seal the tendon (see Fig. 2).

    e. The plate steel is usually A36 steel, galvanized.

5. Stone Joints (Epoxy Joints Between Stones)

    a. In order to install the tendon through the panel, a hole must be drilled from end to end through the panel. Fabrication costs for Indiana limestone dictate that the maximum hole length for volume production is limited to about 1.524 m (5 ft., 0 in.) maximum. This means that a panel will consist of several stones, individually drilled, then assembled end to end with an epoxy joint. This epoxy joint between stones should contain two or more stainless steel dowels spanning the joint. For conservative design, the shear across this joint due to design loads should be carried by the dowels only—not by the epoxy in the joint. The dowels must be epoxied into the drilled holes in the stone to assure proper shear action.

    b. Many epoxy compounds are available for use with stone. The author is partial to Bonstone, Inc., Milwaukee, for use with Indiana limestone.

6. Gravity Connections

Posttensioned panels are usually large and heavy. It is essential, therefore, that particular design attention be given to the gravity connections that attach the panel to the building structure.

    a. One method is to insert a steel angle into the panel. This angle can be bedded against the stone in a full bed of epoxy to provide good load distribution over the stone area (Fig. 3). These long panels must have one end free to slip to accommodate expansion and contraction of panel and structure. This "slip" connection should be designed using bearing pads with a low coefficient of friction. These Teflon pads are available from several manufacturers.

7. Retention Connections

Posttensioned panels commonly span between structural columns. Panels are carried

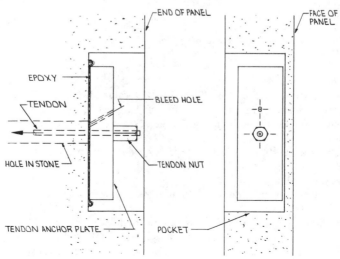

FIG. 2—*Typical detail: tendon anchor plate, posttensioned limestone panel.*

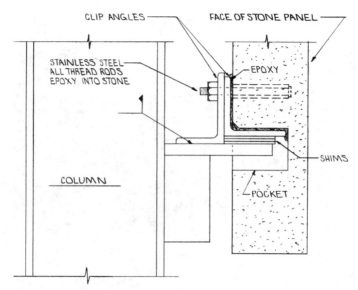

FIG. 3—*Typical detail: gravity connection, posttensioned limestone panel.*

at the columns and retained along the floor line spandrel beam against wind loading. The retention connections along the floor line must be designed to provide vertical movement due to floor deflections and horizontal movement due to differential thermal movement between panel and structure. This can be accomplished with slotted members using slide pads or by various hinged arrangements. These panels are usually quite thick. Expansion bolts, therefore, can be used to provide good retention capability.

8. Stone Stress at Tendon Hole
   Since the panel will have a drilled hole from end to end for the tendon, the panel is substantially weakened along that line. Stone stresses at this point should be carefully checked—especially stresses due to wind loads.

9. Check for Euler Buckling
   Long thin panels should be checked for column buckling due to tendon tension. This is a factor only until the tendon hole is grouted. After the tendon is grouted, Euler Buckling is not a factor.

10. Grouting
    After tendon tensioning, the tendon hole should be pumped full of grout. The grout should be a mixture of nonstaining white cement and water mixed to the consistency of pancake batter. The purpose of the grout is to seal the tendon from oxidation. The grout serves no structural purpose. Never use expanding type grout since the pressure created can split open thin panels.

Fabrication Considerations

1. Epoxy Assembly

The individually drilled stones must be assembled into a complete unit prior to installation of the tendon. The stones should be placed on rollers (or conveyors) in order that good

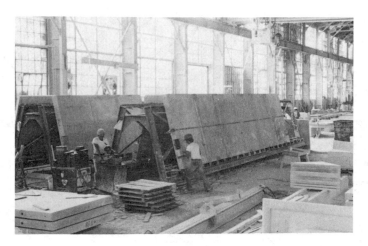

FIG. 4—(top) *Panels assembled in jigs on edge;* (middle) *9.144-m-long panels (30 ft) on truck ready for shipment;* (below) *9.144-m-long panels (30 ft) in storage.*

contact pressure between stones can be obtained during epoxy assembly. The stone should be buttered with epoxy on each end, pushed together, then clamped firmly with long pipe clamps to maintain good epoxy squeeze out during the curing period. Epoxy that sags into the tendon hole should be cleaned with a long swab to provide a clean hole for tendon installation and grout flow. Long thin panels must be assembled on edge since they cannot be lifted from the flat position without seriously overstressing the stone (Fig. 4). After the epoxy between stones has hardened, the tendon anchor plates can be epoxied to the ends of panels using very low tendon pressure (tighten tendon nut using a hand wrench).

2. Tensioning Tendon

The tendon should be tensioned using the manufacturer's hydraulic tensioning equipment. Design tension must be converted to hydraulic gauge readings. In addition, tendon elongation at design tension must be calculated. This elongation must be checked at the required gauge reading in order to validate that the gauge is reading accurately. All gauge readings must be adjusted in accordance with the calibration chart furnished with the gauge.

3. Tendon Grouting

A grouting hole is drilled into the back face of the stone in the center of the panel. This hole intersects the tendon hole. Prior to pumping grout into the tendon hole, the hole should be filled with water and left to soak about half an hour. This wets the walls of the hole and helps to maintain proper grout water content for curing. It also reduces the grout pressure necessary to pump the grout through the hole. The grout pressure gauge must be monitored to keep pressure within allowable limits. Panels have been split open due to high grout pressures.

Handling, Storage, and Transport

1. Handling

Since posttensioned units are usually designed to be supported at the ends, it follows that they should be lifted with slings attached near the ends. This is especially true of units designed with eccentrically located tendons since the "built-in" negative moment will add to any moment resulting from lifting points located toward the centerline of the unit. Units should always be handled in the same attitude as when placed in the building whenever possible. In other words, large flat panels should be handled on edge, etc.

2. Storage and Transport

Units must be stored on two supports only located near each end. Never use more than two support skids for storage or transport. The attitude in storage and transport should be the same as when placed in the building whenever possible (that is, thin panels stored and shipped on edge).

Erection

1. Lifting

The panels should be lifted at two points only located near each end. Lifting clamps are usually not practical because of the clamp sizes and dimension required to handle the large loads. Most projects have been erected using nylon slings. This provides a positive method that requires very little clearance between the structure and the back of the panel. The slings must be used with a spreader bar so that the slings will hang plumb, which prevents sling slippage along the bottom edge of the panel.

2. Storage

Storage at the job site should be on two supports only—the same as in the plant.

Case Histories

The following is a partial list of posttensioned applications utilizing Indiana limestone:

1. 1999 Broadway, Denver, Colorado (1984)
    a. 40-story office building
    b. Panel size—9.144 m by 2.184 m by 15.24 mm (30 ft, 0 in. by 7 ft, 2 in. by 0 ft, 6 in.) thick
    c. Panels span column to column and carry window system
    d. 568 panels required
2. Milestone Tower, Denver, Colorado (1981)
    a. 14-story office building
    b. Panel sizes—9.144 m by 2.134 m by 15.24 mm (30 ft, 0 in. by 7 ft, 0 in. by 0 ft 6 in. thick) 6.096 m by 2.134 m by 15.24 mm (20 ft, 0 in. by 7 ft, 0 in. by 0 ft, 6 in. thick) 4.572 m by 2.134 m by 15.24 m (15 ft, 0 in. by 7 ft, 0 in. by 0 ft, 6 in. thick)
    c. Panels span column to column and carry window system
3. Terrace Tower Two, Denver, Colorado (1985)
    a. 14-story office building
    b. Panel sizes—9.144 m by 2.134 m by 15.24 mm (30 ft, 0 in. by 7 ft, 0 in. by 0 ft, 6 in. thick) 6.096 m by 2.134 m by 15.24 mm (20 ft, 0 in. by 7 ft, 0 in. by 0 ft, 6 in. thick) 4.572 m by 2.134 m by 15.24 mm (15 ft, 0 in. by 7 ft, 0 in. by 0 ft, 6 in. thick)
    c. Panels span column to column and carry window system
    d. 380 panels required
3. Hudson City Bank, Paramus, New Jersey (1977)
    a. 4-story office building
    b. Columns 11.633 m (38 ft, 2 in.) long
    c. 8 required
4. Liggett & Myers World Headquarters, Durham, North Carolina (1976)
    a. Portico addition
    b. 10.668 m by 61 mm by 47 mm (35 ft, 0 in. by 2 ft, 0 in. by 1 ft, 6 1/2 in.) high architrave beam spanning three openings between load-bearing Indiana limestone columns. This beam plus four exposed limestone roof beams carry all loads: roof slab, limestone cornice, limestone balustrade, and coping.
5. Memphis State University, Memphis, Tennessee (1980)
    a. Fine Arts Building addition
    b. Window sills over openings
    c. Sill section size—40.64 mm by 19.37 mm (1 ft, 4 in. by 7 5/8 in. high)
    d. Sill length from 1.829 to 6.311 m (6 to 16 ft)
    e. Sills carry window above
    f. 20 sills required

6. Louisiana State University, Baton Rouge, Louisiana (1976)
   a. Classroom building
   b. Horizontal sunscreens
   c. Section size—38.1 mm by 20.32 mm (1 ft, 3 in. by 8 in. high)
   d. Spans—3.962 m to 5.182 m (13 ft, 0 in. to 17 ft, 0 in.)
   e. 17 required
7. Sixth District Circuit Court Building, Markham, Illinois (1977)
   a. Court building
   b. Railings on pedestals
   c. Railing section—45.72 mm by 60.92 mm (1 ft, 6 in. by 2 ft, 0 in. high)
   d. Spans—6.096 m to 11.278 m (20 ft, 0 in. to 37 ft, 0 in.)
   e. 17 required
8. Security Life Building, Denver, Colorado (1982)
   a. Office building, podium renovation
   b. Panels—5.334 m by 1.829 m by 15.24 mm (17 ft, 6 in. by 6 ft, 0 in. by 0 ft, 6 in.
      thick) 5.334 m by 2.845 m by 15.24 mm (17 ft, 6 in. by 9 ft, 4 in. by 0 ft,
      6 in. thick)
   c. 47 required
9. Highlands School District, Harrison Township, Pennsylvania (1967)
   a. Auditorium
   b. Window mullions at end of auditorium. Glazing installed directly into continuous
      slots cut into stone mullion.
   c. Mullion section 20.32 mm by 45.72 mm (8 in. by 1 ft, 6 in.) deep in the wall
   d. Mullion height—8.331 m (27 ft, 4 in.) clear span
   e. 24 required
10. The Crescent, Dallas, Texas (1985)
    a. Retail office building, and hotel complex
    b. Free standing columns with caps
    c. Column sizes—45.72 mm by 3.048 m (1 ft, 6 in. diameter by 10 ft, 0 in. high)
    d. 8 required
11. Spring Grove Cemetery, Cincinnati, Ohio (1982)
    a. Administration center
    b. Post and beam entrance feature
    c. Columns and beams both posttensioned
12. Labor Department Building, Washington, D.C. (1972)
    a. Limestone railings
    b. Lengths to 3.962 m (13 ft, 0 in.)
    c. 159 required

Maurice Lafayette, Jr.[1]

Stone Veneer and Glass Fiber Reinforced Concrete Panels

REFERENCE: Lafayette, M., Jr.,**"Stone Veneer and Glass Fiber Reinforced Concrete Panels,"** *New Stone Technology, Design, and Construction for Exterior Wall Systems, ASTM STP 996,* B. Donaldson, Ed., American Society for Testing and Materials, Philadelphia, 1988, pp. 128–133.

ABSTRACT: Glass fiber reinforced concrete (GFRC) may be used to replace conventional concrete backup to stone veneer precast panels, thereby producing a lightweight panel. Toe-in spring clips connect stone veneer to GFRC backup. A bondbreaker separates the GFRC and stone veneer to allow differential movement. A steel stud frame commonly functions as a panel stiffener. The stud frame is attached to the GFRC skin by means of flex anchors.

The gravity load of the GFRC skin is transferred to the stud frame by two methods: (1) flex anchors only, and (2) gravity anchors in addition to flex anchors. The stud frame is attached to the building structural frame, and the loads of the panel are carried through the stud frame to the panel connection points on the structure.

KEY WORDS: bondbreaker, cladding, curing, flex anchors, glass fiber reinforced concrete, gravity anchors, steel stud frame, stiffeners, spring clip, stone veneer, wire connectors

Over the past 13 years an exciting new architectural cladding panel system has been developed called GFRC (Glass Fiber Reinforced Concrete).

GFRC is a lightweight wall panel system with similar architectural characteristics to precast concrete. The system has rapidly developed in the United States and is used primarily for architectural wall panels. The success is due to the capability to provide a high-quality wall system with a wide range of shapes, colors, and texture. GFRC also has the capability to support a stone veneer, and, over the past five years, several projects in the United States have been completed. A GFRC panel consists of a stone veneer anchored to a GFRC substrate, which is then attached to a steel support frame. The GFRC panel system with a stone veneer has a weight of approximately 28 psf (1.3 kPa).

Glass fiber reinforced concrete is the term applied to portland cement–based composites manufactured, in the case of panels, by the spray-up process using special alkali-resistant glass fibers, typically 5% by weight of the total mix, which are chopped into lengths of 1 1/2 to 2 in. (38 to 51 mm) and sprayed into a form with an appropriate cement/aggregate slurry. It is important to understand that the material is a composite with reinforcing elements (fibers) randomly distributed throughout the matrix, unlike reinforced concrete where the reinforcing steel is placed primarily in the tensile stress area. [The properties of GFRC as a material and design of the GFRC panel system are not discussed in this paper; the reader is referred to Ref. *1* for more information.]

[1] President, Lafayette Manufacturing, Inc., Hayward, CA 94545.

Stone and Anchorage Selection

Granite, marble, slate, and travertine natural cut stones have been used, starting in about 1983, as veneers covering the entire panel or as feature strips on GFRC panels.

Stone thicknesses used by GFRC producers have varied from 1/2 to 1 1/4 in. (1.27 to 3 cm). The length of the stone has varied up to 7 ft (2.1 m) with a width of up to 5 ft (1.5 m) for a maximum area of 35 ft² (3.25 m²), while the minimum has been a 1 ft, 4 in. (0.41 m) square stone. However, Lafayette Manufacturing, Inc. recommends a minimum stone thickness of 7/8 in. (2 cm) with a maximum of 1 1/4 in. (3 cm) when using a GFRC backup.

Typically the stone veneer is mechanically fastened to the GFRC skin with a stainless steel wire connector (spring clip). Holes are drilled in the stone veneer on a 45° angle from the horizontal and are preferably 3/4 to 1 1/4 in. (19 to 32 mm) deep but no closer than 1/8 in. (3 mm) from the face of the stone. The connectors are oriented horizontally on vertical walls.

There are two recommended stone anchor details used by GFRC producers, both of which use a toe-in spring clip. (See Figs. 1 and 2 for details of these preferred anchor details.) The spring clips are Type 302 or 304 stainless steel with a diameter of 5/32 in. (4 mm) or 3/16 in. (4.8 mm) and are the same as those used in veneer-faced precast concrete panels. The anchors are spaced a maximum of 24 in. (0.61 m) on center or one anchor for every 2 ft² (0.19 m²) of stone veneer, depending on the flexural strength of the stone. Anchors should be no closer than 6 in. (15 cm) to the edge of the stone with a minimum of three anchors per stone. The minimum ratio of service to test load should be at least 5.

The GFRC and the stone veneer must be allowed to move independently from one another due to differential shrinkage. Both spring clip anchors are designed to flex.

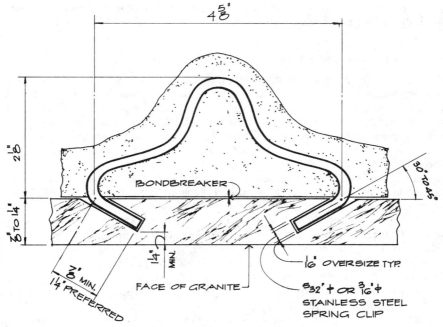

FIG. 1—*Stone anchor detail.*

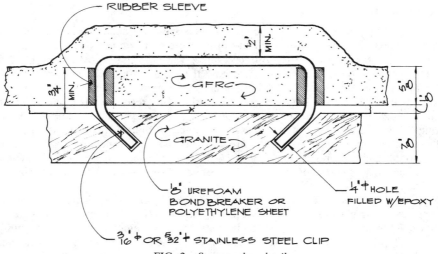

FIG. 2—*Stone anchor detail.*

The designed flexibility on the anchor shown in Fig. 1 is the ability of the clip to move within the 1/8-in. (3.2-mm) oversize hole in the stone veneer. The designed flexibility in the anchor shown in Fig. 2 is the addition of a rubber sleeve added to the spring clip. The clip is allowed to flex within the rubber sleeve space. An applied bondbreaker to the backside of the stone veneer and the flexibility of the spring clip anchor allows for adequate differential movement. The bondbreaker may be a 6-mil polyethylene film or may be a 1/8-in. (3.2-mm) polyethylene foam pad.

GFRC Panel Production Process

The production process consists of first placing the stone veneer (with anchors already installed) face down in the form with rubber spacers between each unit. The joint sizes between the stone veneer may vary 1/4 to 3/4 in. (6 to 19 mm). Next, the joints between the stone and the perimeter of the form are sealed with tape to prevent any of the GFRC slurry from running onto the face of the stone. The bondbreaker is then applied to cover the entire stone veneer surface. The unit now is ready to receive the spray application of GFRC.

Simultaneous sprays of cement/sand water slurry and chopped glass fibers are deposited from a hand-held spray gun onto the back of the stone in the form. The GFRC composite usually uses an acrylic thermoplastic copolymer dispersion as an admixture to eliminate the necessity of moist curing. In addition, a curing compound may be sprayed on the back of the GFRC panel to prevent moisture loss during overnight curing.

Roller compaction ensures conformation with the back of the stone and removal of entrapped air. Spraying and compaction continue until the required typical 5/8 to 3/4 in. (16 to 19 mm) material thickness is reached. The GFRC composite is also hand packed a minimum of 1/2 in. (13 mm) over the spring clip anchor. The overlay material is worked by hand into the wet GFRC skin.

GFRC properties are such that, unless the panel has a functionally convenient shape, stiffeners are required for panels to be of appreciable size. Stiffeners may be prefabricated, plant-attached cold-formed steel studs or upstanding single skin ribs formed on the back of the panel or integral ribs formed on the back of the panel by spraying over hidden rib formers, such as expanded polystyrene strips. Either method stiffens and reinforces the GFRC skin and provides a means for connection to the supporting structure.

While each has its own advantages, the steel stud frame is usually the more economical and preferred method for stiffening in the United States except where the steel stud may be exposed to the weather or where complex shapes dictate the use of self-formed stiffeners (ribs). The attachment of the skin to the steel stud is via a flex anchor. These flex anchors are prewelded to the steel stud and bonded to the skin with additional GFRC material called a bonding pad. The area of this bonding pad is approximately 18 to 32 in.^{2} (11.6 to 20.6 by 103 mm^2).

The thin GFRC skin is adequate to support the induced wind and dead loads as it functions only to transfer the stone veneer loads to the steel stud frame.

Currently there are two methods of transferring the gravity load of the skin to the steel frame. One method uses only flex anchors to transfer the gravity load of the skin to the stud frame. The flex anchor carries the weight of the GFRC skin elastically, yet flexes to compensate for the volumetric changes of the skin. This is only recommended for very small panels. The preferred system with stone veneer GFRC panels uses gravity anchors in addition to the flex anchor. Both methods transfer wind load through the flex anchors to the steel stud frame.

The most common flex anchor used is a smooth round rod. Diameter choice is influenced by the dimension from the skin to the stud and whether or not there is a separate gravity anchor. It is welded with groove welds at the top for flexibility. The anchor must be of ample rigidity and strength to carry its tributary gravity and wind load while remaining flexible enough not to restrain the skin against thermal or moisture movements. A plastic sleeve may be put over the anchor foot to minimize restraint. Also, the orientation of the foot of the anchor is usually towards the center of the panel to reduce restraint due to GFRC shrinkage.

In the gravity anchor system, anchors are provided to transfer the weight of the skin to the frame. The flex anchor in this system can be smaller [1/4 in. (6 mm) minimum diameter] and provide less in-plane restraint since it does not carry the vertical dead load of the GFRC skin. Generally, a minimum of two gravity anchors are provided. For example, the flat plate tee anchor system has its stem plate welded at one end to the stud and at the other to the cross plate which is attached to the skin similar to the flex anchor (see Fig. 3). By adjusting the stem height and thickness, strength is achieved in one direction without sacrifice of flexibility in the other.

With the flat plate tee gravity anchor, the studs may be reinforced by adding additional plates or adding another stud. With the trussed round bar gravity anchor, as shown in Fig. 4, the studs do not generally need to be reinforced. These gravity anchors are usually at every stud, and the resulting loads can be supported by a "C" stud without additional strengthening.

The in-plane rigidity of the skin transfers its weight directly to the gravity anchors. In seismic areas one, not both, of the gravity anchors can be designed to take in-plane horizontal forces. This may require increasing the vertical capacity of the other to carry the rotational forces due to the distance between the center of the skins' mass and the resisting connections.

The stud frame is attached to the building structural frame, and the loads of the panel are carried through the stud frame to the panel connection points on the structure. These locations are coordinated between the architect, structural engineer, and GFRC manufacturer during the design of the project. It is important to have the structural frame and GFRC panel compatible so that the engineer can design the building frame and the GFRC manufacturer can design the panel connections.

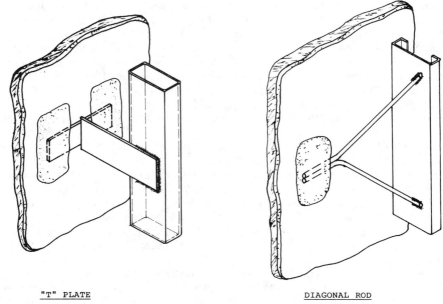

"T" PLATE   DIAGONAL ROD

FIG. 3—*Isometric.*

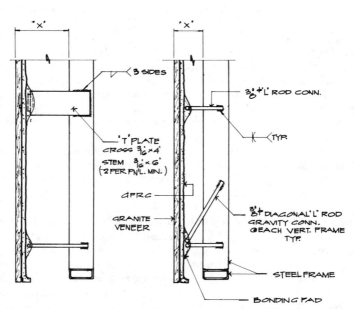

FIG. 4—*"T" plate and diagonal rod gravity connection detail.* NOTE: *the gravity connective function is to transfer the load of the GFRC skin back to the steel frame where dimension "X" exceeds 3 in.*

After initial overnight curing, the panel is removed from the form and placed in an environment where it is exposed to a temperature above 60°F (16°C) for at least seven days prior to shipment to the job site.

The use of a steel frame allows for the design of relatively large unit sizes that can be efficient and cost-effective to manufacture and install. Units range from 20 ft (6.1 m) in length to 13 ft (4 m) in height. The attachments of the panels to the structure are usually accomplished by two load-bearing connections and a minimum of two lateral connections.

The cavity between the steel studs is often used for placement of the building insulation and for electrical, mechanical, and plumbing cases.

GFRC is a very adaptable wall panel system that, because of its lightweight feature, offers to the architect today new and imaginative way to design exterior wall cladding panels that were not possible in the past.

For further information on production, quality control, and design, refer to Ref. *1*.

References

[*1*] "Recommended Practice for Glass Fiber Reinforced Concrete Panels," Prestressed Concrete Institute, Chicago, IL, 1987.

Adhered Thin Stone Veneer Systems

William Loper[1] and Thomas Obermeier[2]

Thin Stone Veneers—A Steel/Silicone Diaphragm System

REFERENCE: Loper, W. and Obermeier, T., **"Thin Stone Veneers—A Steel/Silicone Diaphragm System,"** *New Stone Technology, Design, and Construction for Exterior Wall Systems, ASTM STP 996,* B. Donaldson, Ed., American Society for Testing and Materials, Philadelphia, 1988, pp. 137–140.

ABSTRACT: Stone utilization and fabrication has evolved rapidly in recent years. Originally, stone was a massive structural building material. Today, with the use of sophisticated cutting techniques, stone can be a thin veneer cladding for building exteriors. To utilize this thin stone product a number of prefabricated panel systems have appeared including the Cygnus steel/silicone diaphragm system. The Cygnus system utilizes structural silicone to uniformly distribute the exterior dead and dynamic loads over a galvanized steel diaphragm panel. This patented, proprietary manufactured system provides a tough, durable, light-weight exterior skin utilizing stone, tile, aluminum, or glass exterior cladding material.

KEY WORDS: steel/silicone diaphragm, cygnus panel system, thin veneers

Stone as a building material originally was utilized primarily on bearing wall or post and lintel construction. The Parthenon, Stonehenge, and H. H. Richardson's Marshall Field warehouse in Chicago are fine historical testimonies to this building technique, that is, stone used as a massive, substantial, and worthy material.

In the mid-nineteenth century, building techniques for tall structures evolved. The Brooklyn Bridge, the Eiffel Tower, the Crystal Palace, and in stone Louis Sullivan's ten-story Wainwright building in St. Louis utilized structural metal frames; concrete frames for tall structures were soon to follow. Stone, the massive, substantial worthy material, was no longer holding the building up, but more modestly holding the weather out. This worthy material's function had changed. It had no need of thickness; in fact, thickness was a liability for a material whose function was to curtain the interior from the exterior. The now thinner exterior skin had the obvious advantage of providing more usable space within the building and required the structure to support less weight. The concrete or steel frame did the structural work; the stone was relegated to the role of cosmetic skin. Architects and designers have struggled with the aesthetic expression of this new thin stone cladding.

Subsequently, stone fabrication evolved again. With this evolution came more sophisticated saws providing better cutting technique and greater dimensional control. Sizeable pieces of stone are now available 1-cm thick. For exteriors, the once traditional 7-cm-thick stone weighed 180 kg/m². The now available 1 and 2-cm materials weigh 25.6 and 51.2 kg/m², respectively. This now thin but still worthy, exciting material has two attendant problems, how best to express it aesthetically and how to hang it functionally.

The first of these problems is basically beyond the scope of this paper except to report

[1] President, Cygnus, Inc., Denver, CO 80203.
[2] Consultant, 1580 Lincoln, Denver, CO 80203.

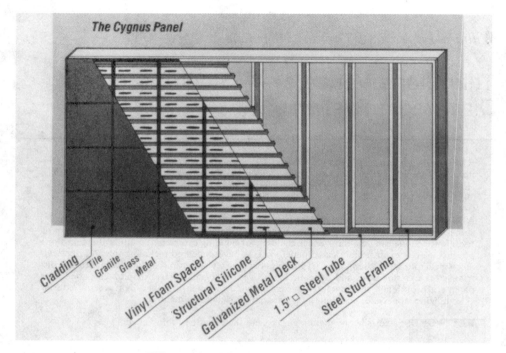

The Cygnus Panel

Cladding — Tile — Granite — Glass — Metal — Vinyl Foam Spacer — Structural Silicone — Galvanized Metal Deck — 1.5″ □ Steel Tube — Steel Stud Frame

FIG. 1—*The steel/silicone diaphragm system.*

that the tools for solving this aesthetic dilemma would appear to be color, texture, and pattern as opposed to the expression of thickness. The stone can be fabricated in various finishes, honed, flamed, polished, and others, and can be arranged in patterns and designs combining color and texture. Architects, designers, and building owners increasingly recognize inherent economic and problem-free advantages of flush exterior skins and rely on color, texture, and pattern to enrich their design. The now thin but still worthy stone works well in these patterned, substantially flush, curtain wall systems.

To solve the market's impulse to utilize this thin stone product, we find a proliferation of panel systems. These systems include:

1. Precast concrete.
2. Glass fiber reinforced concrete (GFRC).
3. Truss or strongback (considered conventional).
4. Stucco and backer board.
5. Steel/silicone diaphragm.

Consideration of these industrialized factory-manufactured systems should include the following:

1. Weight and thickness of skin.
2. Structural connections.
3. Structural loads (dynamic and static).
4. Panel shape and design potential.
5. Thermal expansion and contraction.

6. Seismic loading.
7. Water and/or air penetration.
8. Durability of components.
9. Single source building skin responsibility.
10. Safety factors.
11. Building code considerations.
12. Quality assurance.

The steel/silicone diaphragm system, in production since 1981 with over 75 structures completed or in progress, addresses the above considerations in a unique manner. The system (see Fig. 1) is composed of a nonload-bearing, steel stud frame to which 22-gauge 3.81-cm hot dipped galvanized steel decking is screw attached. Frost-proof cladding (ceramic tile, granite, limestone, or marble suitable for exterior cladding) is spaced 0.3175 cm from the decking with vinyl foam tape and attached to the galvanized decking with structural silicone, a material that can accommodate 50% movement while carrying tensile loads of 1.36 kg/cm² (20 psi), including a 4 to 1 safety factor. The silicone distributes the loads on the cladding in a uniform pattern, thus avoiding point loads and concentrated stress conditions. The structural silicone is applied in quantities so the unit shear stress does not exceed 0.068 kg/cm² (1 psi). A mechanical fastener (see Fig. 2) designed according to Uniform

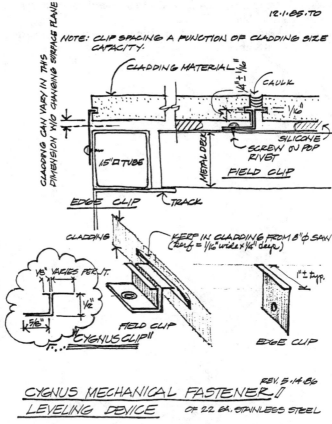

FIG. 2—*Cygnus mechanical fastener leveling device.*

Building Code requirements may be used in conjunction with the silicone if a second, load-carrying system is desired or if the weight of the stone makes the handling of shear stresses by the silicone a less economic use of the material. Such a composite connection system utilizes the mechanical fasteners for dead loads and the silicone for dynamic wind loading in a manner similar to the now familiar structural glazing phenomenon. The mechanical fastener may also aid in leveling the exterior face of the selected cladding. Once the cladding is adhered to the panel, the joints in the cladding material are factory caulked with the same structural silicone.

The galvanized steel substrate may be designed and installed to function as a secondary water barrier if the integrity of the cladding with reference to water permeability is in question.

The components when assembled combine frost-proof cladding, galvanized steel, and structural silicone to form a very tough durable diaphragm panel. This panel adjusts easily to a building's concrete or steel frame. Its integral light weight and resiliency handle wind, thermal, seismic, and appropriate structural loading nicely.

A word of caution. The thin stone veneers must be appropriate as cladding. A battery of ASTM tests for compressive strength, modulus of rupture, absorption, density, and abrasion resistance exist as standards. Information is also available regarding physical properties such as thermal expansion, modulus of elasticity, shear strength, and tensile strength. Freeze/thaw durability, water permeability, and cladding consistency are also considerations. Once an appropriate cladding is selected, the steel/silicone diaphragm system will insure a first class panel and exterior skin.

The steel/silicone diaphragm is a patented, proprietary system, thus assuring its availability from qualified, professional sources.

Richard C. Wood[1]

Rediscovering Marble and Natural Stone

REFERENCE: Wood, R. C., **"Rediscovering Marble and Natural Stone,"** *New Stone Technology, Design, and Construction for Exterior Wall Systems, ASTM STP 996*, B. Donaldson, Ed., American Society for Testing and Materials, Philadelphia, 1988, pp. 141–151.

ABSTRACT: This paper deals with the application of thin-gauged marble and natural stone on the exteriors of buildings. The paper presents several methods of doing this, such as site applied over concrete and masonry surfaces and over lightweight steel studs using a wire-reinforced, latex modified mortar system.

The paper also presents the latest technology in exterior cladding utilizing lightweight steel panels, constructed off site where marble or natural stone may be applied to portland cement boards with a latex polymer modified mortar adhesive system. Detailed drawings of the applications are included as well as photographs of projects in various stages of construction.

KEY WORDS: exterior cladding, marble cladding, stone cladding, marble panels, stone panels, veneer cladding

Natural stone and marble offer a variety of colors, texture and dimensions, and outstanding durability. They exemplify the look of classic elegance. For the building owner, stone represents an image of quality and success.

All this is well and good, but what about the cost? And what about the time for installation of these materials? Too often too many of the architect's clients have marble tastes and a concrete pocketbook.

So, how does the architect satisfy his clients' desires without sacrificing appearance, quality, and the durability of that appearance?

Let us review a project in the Western United States in which the building owner wanted a granite-clad building. The architect said, "No problem" and went about the business of determining client needs, site selection, and conceptual plans. He then gave the client his estimate of the building costs. When the client regained consciousness it was determined that the full granite exterior had to go.

To make a long story very short, instead of using a full thick granite, a thin 15-mm granite was set on this 15-story building installed with a latex mortar system, and the architect was able to give the client what he wanted well *within budget* and *without sacrifice* to quality or durability.

Herb McLaughlin (Kaplan, McLaughlin and Diaz, Architects) told a similar story when he said that the only way he could meet the client's needs within budget was to use a thin granite glued in place. Mr. McLaughlin also said that he was not very confident of the durability of a glued-up piece of stone.

This is a major concern to architects, building code officials, and building owners. Largely, this feeling of insecurity with "glued-on systems" stems from two sources: (1) a lack of awareness of the many projects successfully fabricated in this manner; and (2) a bad experience with a project where improper or inferior materials were utilized.

[1] Director of Marketing, Laticrete International Inc., Bethany, CT 06525.

Once an architect has been selected for a project, his objectives are four-fold: (1) to give the client what he needs and wants; (2) to stay within the allotted budget for both time and money; (3) to provide a system that works and lasts, whether we're talking about exterior facades or doorknobs; and (4) to provide all of the above within the bounds of energy requirements, building codes, and local conditions.

Looking at exterior thin stone and marble facades, we can accomplish these objectives in a variety of ways depending on the structure, the timing, the finish desired, and the budget.

We must look for systems that are specifically designed for the intended use. In the case of installation systems for thin stone and marble veneers, we must look for materials that are designed to bond to these specific veneers while maintaining resiliency and long-term durability. The materials must also continue to perform adequately throughout the intended life of the building.

It is important to look at the history of successful thin stone and marble installations. This system is not by any means new. It has a 30-year history of proven success in many climates when the *proper* materials are specified and used.

The first project which illustrates this point is the Florida Bank Building, constructed in 1964. Here the architect was able to utilize both polished and split-face marble material,

WALL — EXTERIOR or INTERIOR
TILE OVER MASONRY
Drawing No. 104.01

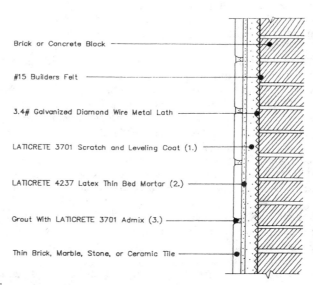

Brick or Concrete Block

#15 Builders Felt

3.4# Galvanized Diamond Wire Metal Lath

LATICRETE 3701 Scratch and Leveling Coat (1.)

LATICRETE 4237 Latex Thin Bed Mortar (2.)

Grout With LATICRETE 3701 Admix (3.)

Thin Brick, Marble, Stone, or Ceramic Tile

NOTES:

1.) 1:3 Portland Cement/Masons Sand Gauged With LATICRETE 3701 Admix At 1/2" − 3/4" (12mm − 19mm) Thick or As Required To Plumb Wall Surface

2.) 1:1 Portland Cement/Fine Sand Gauged With LATICRETE 4237 Additive

3.) LATICRETE Grout Gauged With LATICRETE 3701 Admix

4.) Refer To Specification Data Sheet No. 230.6 For Complete Installation Details

FIG. 1—*Thin application of marble or stone directly over masonry wall.*

FIG. 2—*Florida Bank Building, constructed in 1964 using the Laticrete system to install large 2 by 3-ft marble as well as 2 by 8-in. pieces of split face marble directly over concrete block walls.*

FIG. 3—*Gold Hill Square in Singapore, a two-story high rise, was completely surfaced with 2 by 8-in. split face marble with the Laticrete system directly over slip formed concrete.*

EXTERIOR or INTERIOR WALL
CERAMIC TILE ON CONCRETE
Drawing No. 104.2

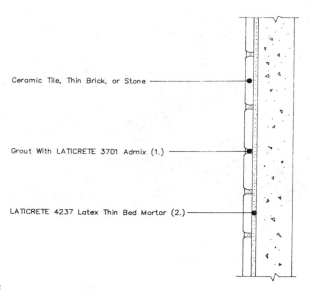

Ceramic Tile, Thin Brick, or Stone

Grout With LATICRETE 3701 Admix (1.)

LATICRETE 4237 Latex Thin Bed Mortar (2.)

NOTES:
1.) LATICRETE Grout Gauged With LATICRETE 3701 Admix
2.) 1:1 Portland Cement/Fine Sand Gauged With LATICRETE 4237 Additive
3.) Refer To Specification Data Sheet No. 230.41 For Complete Details

FIG. 4—*Thin application of marble or stone directly over concrete.*

which creates an interesting contrast of textures. The installation methods for both types of material were identical. On one side of the building, relatively small 5 by 14-cm pieces of split-face marble were adhered to a block wall while the opposite side utilized large pieces of 0.7-m by 1-m by 9-mm marble. All marble was installed by applying a latex polymer modified sand and cement mortar to the wall and back buttering the marble prior to its installation (Fig. 1).

This project has withstood constant thermal shock subjecting the face material to temperature variations greater than 100°F (37.8°C). Today the project looks as good as it did 23 years ago (Fig. 2).

A similar application can be seen on The Goldhill Square project (Fig. 3) in Singapore. On this project, large and small split face units of marble were installed using a latex modified sand and cement mortar directly over slip formed concrete (Fig. 4).

Let's take a moment here to see what exactly the latex modified cement setting material is doing to ensure the success of these types of applications. It is well understood that cement, in the presence of moisture, will hydrate or, in other words, grow fingers to bond it to other particles and make a very strong structural material.

Sand is generally added to the mixture because the cement will have a tendency to shrink as it hydrates, and the sand provides bulk so that the particles of cement will form around them and not cause a bonding failure due to excessive cement shrinkage. A setting mix created by sand, cement, and water is very brittle and would have a tendency to break under

FIG. 5—*Miller residence, New York City, 12 by 12 by 5/8-in.-thick granite installed over steel studs and wire-reinforced mortar bed using the Laticrete system. An economical, easily installed remodeling system.*

differential movement between the surfacing material and the substrate. The Laticrete material is a very specially formulated synthetic rubber polymer that encapsulates the particles of sand and cement and controls the hydration process, ensuring the quality of the hydration. In addition, because the synthetic rubber has encapsulated these particles of sand and cement, the cured mortar is now made up of three elements: sand, cement, and rubber. The result is a very resilient mix with 400% greater strength than normal setting mixes and a far greater resiliency.

Let's now look at a somewhat smaller project involving the remodeling of an existing brownstone residence in New York City (Fig. 5). Here a steel stud and wire-reinforced setting bed formed the substrate for the application of 30 by 30 cm pieces of granite. The granite was set in place using the same procedures we have already discussed, latex modified sand and cement setting material thinly applied to both the substrate and the back of the granite pieces (Fig. 6).

We have briefly reviewed thin marble and stone applications on a number of different substrates in a number of different climatic zones. Common to the success of all of these projects has been the high strength and resilient system of installation.

Still, some believe "If it ain't bolted, it ain't gonna stay!" Historical evidence and extensive independent laboratory tests indicate that a thin stone veneer properly installed with the right materials will perform as well, look as well, last as long, and cost a fraction as much as conventionally anchored systems.

Phillip Johnson commented some years ago that: "The first thing an architect must be

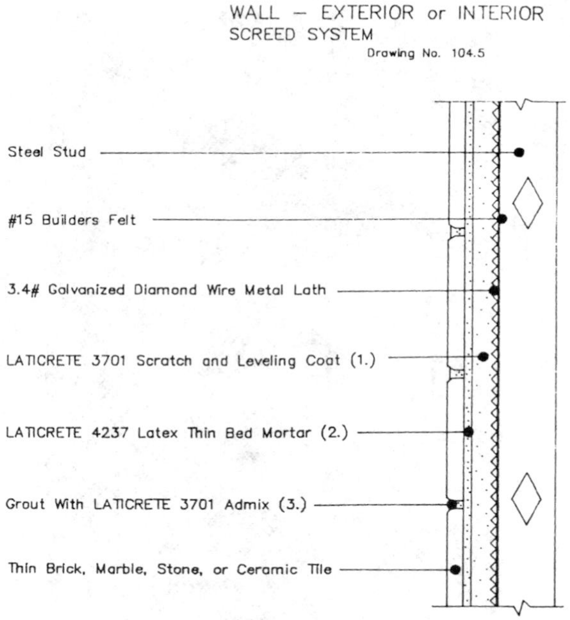

WALL — EXTERIOR or INTERIOR
SCREED SYSTEM
Drawing No. 104.5

Steel Stud

#15 Builders Felt

3.4# Galvanized Diamond Wire Metal Lath

LATICRETE 3701 Scratch and Leveling Coat (1.)

LATICRETE 4237 Latex Thin Bed Mortar (2.)

Grout With LATICRETE 3701 Admix (3.)

Thin Brick, Marble, Stone, or Ceramic Tile

NOTES:

1.) 1:3 Portland Cement/Masons Sand Gauged With LATICRETE 3701 Admix At 1/2" — 3/4" (12 — 19mm) Thick
2.) 1:1 Portland Cement/Fine Sand Gauged With LATICRETE 4237 Additive
3.) LATICRETE Grout Gauged With LATICRETE 3701 Admix
4.) Refer To Specification Data Sheet No. 230.6 For Complete Installation Details

FIG. 6—*Thin application of marble or stone over wire lath to steel studs.*

FIG. 7—*Lightweight panelized project enclosed from bare steel to finished enclosure in one week.*

FIG. 8—*Laticrete Panel System (LPS) being fabricated in the controlled conditions of the panel fabrication shop.*

LATICRETE PANEL SYSTEM

<u>ROOF DETAIL</u>

DRAWING NO. 101.11

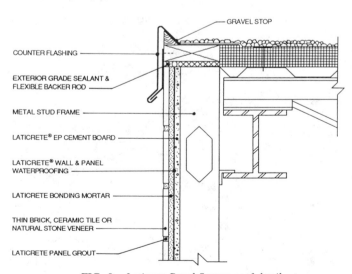

GRAVEL STOP

COUNTER FLASHING

EXTERIOR GRADE SEALANT & FLEXIBLE BACKER ROD

METAL STUD FRAME

LATICRETE® EP CEMENT BOARD

LATICRETE® WALL & PANEL WATERPROOFING

LATICRETE BONDING MORTAR

THIN BRICK, CERAMIC TILE OR NATURAL STONE VENEER

LATICRETE PANEL GROUT

FIG. 9—*Laticrete Panel System roof detail.*

LATICRETE PANEL SYSTEM

SPANDREL PANEL DETAIL

DRAWING NO. 101.12

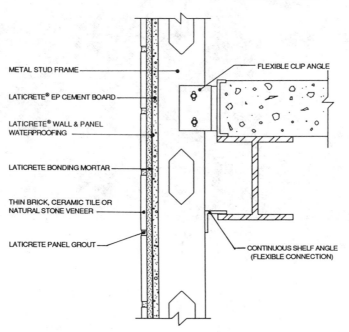

METAL STUD FRAME

LATICRETE® EP CEMENT BOARD

LATICRETE® WALL & PANEL WATERPROOFING

LATICRETE BONDING MORTAR

THIN BRICK, CERAMIC TILE OR NATURAL STONE VENEER

LATICRETE PANEL GROUT

FLEXIBLE CLIP ANGLE

CONTINUOUS SHELF ANGLE (FLEXIBLE CONNECTION)

FIG. 10—*Laticrete Panel System spandrel detail.*

LATICRETE PANEL SYSTEM

WINDOW HEAD & SILL DETAIL

DRAWING NO. 101.13

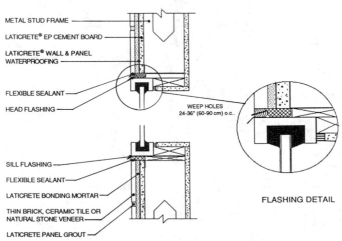

METAL STUD FRAME

LATICRETE® EP CEMENT BOARD

LATICRETE® WALL & PANEL WATERPROOFING

FLEXIBLE SEALANT

HEAD FLASHING

WEEP HOLES
24-36" (60-90 cm) o.c..

SILL FLASHING

FLEXIBLE SEALANT

LATICRETE BONDING MORTAR

THIN BRICK, CERAMIC TILE OR NATURAL STONE VENEER

LATICRETE PANEL GROUT

FLASHING DETAIL

FIG. 11—*Laticrete Panel System window head and sill detail.*

concerned with is getting a job!'' Giving the client what he wants within his budget and within his time frame is a great way to not only get the job, but also to create a very happy client.

Let's now look more closely at a specific project, the time frames involved, and the specific cost (Fig. 7). This project was enclosed from bare steel to finished walls in one week. The panels were constructed off site (Fig. 8), delivered to the project, and erected with a minimum of on-site labor and without need of any form of scaffolding. The completed wall was installed at less than $18 per square foot, well within time and budget.

This structure used a state-of-the art, lightweight panel system weighing less than 15 pounds per square foot. The entire assembly was designed and tested to withstand thermal shock, physical shock, wind loading (both negative and positive), and to resist wind-driven rain up to 100 miles per hour.[2] While not as critical in a two-story building, the light weight of the panels will generally mean lighter steel and/or less concrete. Not only can weight saving be an important cost consideration, but for a structure being built on existing foundations every pound of dead load becomes critical.

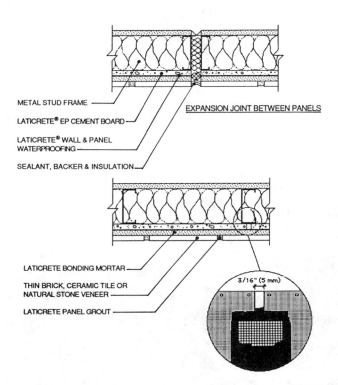

LATICRETE PANEL SYSTEM

JOINT TREATMENT DETAILS

DRAWING NO. 101.14

METAL STUD FRAME

LATICRETE® EP CEMENT BOARD

LATICRETE® WALL & PANEL WATERPROOFING

SEALANT, BACKER & INSULATION

EXPANSION JOINT BETWEEN PANELS

LATICRETE BONDING MORTAR

THIN BRICK, CERAMIC TILE OR NATURAL STONE VENEER

LATICRETE PANEL GROUT

3/16" (5 mm)

JOINT TREATMENT @ SEAM BETWEEN BOARDS

FIG. 12—*Laticrete Panel System joint treatment details.*

---

[2] Construction Consulting Laboratories test report available upon written request.

LATICRETE PANEL SYSTEM

1-1/2 HOUR FIRE-RATED WALL DESIGN

DRAWING NO. 101.15

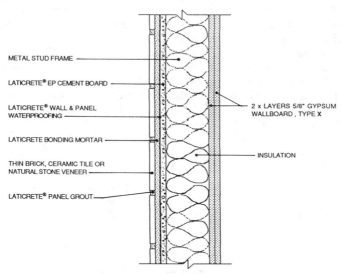

METAL STUD FRAME

LATICRETE® EP CEMENT BOARD

LATICRETE® WALL & PANEL WATERPROOFING

LATICRETE BONDING MORTAR

THIN BRICK, CERAMIC TILE OR NATURAL STONE VENEER

LATICRETE® PANEL GROUT

2 x LAYERS 5/8" GYPSUM WALLBOARD , TYPE X

INSULATION

FIG. 13—*Laticrete Panel System 1 1/2 h fire-rated wall design.*

FIG. 14—*The finished project clad with the Laticrete Panel System ready for the client, on time and within budget.*

The construction of the panel is comprised of 50 by 150-mm 16-gauge steel studs over which a high-density portland cement building board is applied, followed by a (high-bond) waterproof membrane coating to resist water penetration on the panel. Once the surface preparation has been accomplished, the traditional method of a latex modified sand cement mortar is applied to the face of the panel and a latex modified grout is utilized to finish the job (Figs. 9–13). The result (Fig. 14) is an attractive-looking structure that was fabricated in off-site, controlled conditions, erected on the job in a minimum of time, and provided the building owner with the look he desired at a cost well within his budget.

Whether we use a negative cast system where the panel is actually constructed upside down, a wire and mortar system, whether we apply stone on the job site or off site on panels or whether we construct load-bearing walls or ultra lightweight panels, this can be successfully accomplished and has been accomplished with over 30 years of field-proven performance in many climatic zones around the world.

Quality materials from reputable manufacturers willing to guarantee their systems, installed by competent mechanics, can bring the magnificient look of natural marble and granite back into the reach of more of today's building owners. And last, with the infinite variety of colors and textures available in thin marble and granite and the flexibility of application offered by quality polymer modified sand and cement mortars, there is virtually no end to the look and feeling that can be created to meet the needs and desires of today's building owners.

Curtain Wall Framed Systems

Gordon H. Smith[1]

Exterior Wall Systems Performance and Design Criteria: Should These Vary with Different Types of Cladding Systems— Glass Fiber Reinforced Cement, Stone, Metal, Glass—Panel, Frame, or Veneer?

REFERENCE: Smith, G. H., **"Exterior Wall Systems Performance and Design Criteria: Should These Vary with Different Types of Cladding Systems—Glass Fiber Reinforced Cement, Stone, Metal, Glass—Panel, Frame, or Veneer?,"** *New Stone Technology, Design, and Construction for Exterior Wall Systems, ASTM STP 996*, B. Donaldson, Ed., American Society for Testing and Materials, Philadelphia, 1988, pp. 155–159.

ABSTRACT: This paper will discuss the difference between performance criteria and design criteria, how performance criteria can affect selection of material and support system, and how each different material and support system may have different design criteria which must be addressed.

This paper will present an overview of the subject keyed into specific project experiences and is intended to serve as a reminder of topics to be addressed by designer in material and system selection and construction document preparation.

KEY WORDS: exterior wall systems, cladding

Often when sitting down at an initial meeting with a client who is considering the possible use of stone as a cladding material or who has already determined that the facade for his building will include stone as one of the cladding materials, I find that attention is focused on the architectural selection of a particular stone too early in the design process.

While aesthetics certainly are an important criteria in the selection of the particular stone, the selection process should also address the performance requirements for the overall facade, the type of cladding systems which can meet these requirements, and, if stone is selected, the type of support system best suited to the aesthetic and functional requirements of the building at hand.

All facades must be capable of: (1) withstanding the anticipated design wind pressure; (2) controlling air infiltration; (3) resisting water penetration; (4) withstanding the effects of temperature changes; and (5) accommodating movement of the building frame. Before selecting a cladding system or a cladding support system, such as a truss system to support stone, one must evaluate the specific parameters in each category for the project under consideration, as well as the specific performance capabilities of a particular stone being evaluated.

[1] President, Gordon H. Smith Corp., Exterior Walls Consultants, New York, NY 10016.

Technical Discussion

The following is a review of each category of criteria and how it impacts upon the individual facade type and building cladding materials.

1. A facade must be capable of resisting wind pressure, and thus, regardless of material or support system, the appropriate design wind pressure for the building, based on its shape and location, must be determined. This determination is made by employing a multiplicity of tools available to the design team. These include local code requirements, ANSI Standard A-58.1 "Minimum Design Wind Loads for Buildings and Other Structures," a wind tunnel study, and the individual designer's experience. When determined in a timely manner, knowing the loads which must be resisted can aid the designer in making an informed decision on cladding system selection, cladding support system selection, individual stone selection, and, in particular, stone thickness versus support method. Two or four-sided support, glazing in, kerf support, drilled-in wedge or wire anchors, glued-in bent pins, etc. all have individual advantages and disadvantages. For example, large size thin stones are more readily useable in glued-in pin, drilled-in wedge, or wire anchor supported systems to resist high wind loads than would a glazed-in or kerf support system. Stone thickness, to provide adequate strength in a glazed-in or kerf system, is determined by strength of the individual stone versus the joint pattern which will govern the stone span—height and width. In a "back-anchored system" such as glued-in pins, drilled-in wedge, or wire anchors, the relationship of the cost of thicker stone versus the cost of an additional anchor will govern.

When considering an aluminum support system, the designer must keep in mind the differing deflection limitations of the materials being supported. When supporting an aluminum panel or glass lite, convention has it that the allowable deflection of the supporting element can be as much as $L/175$, not to exceed 3/4 in. In higher quality projects, the deflection limitation is often reduced to $L/240$, not to exceed 3/4 in. Glass manufacturers' strength charts are based upon rigid support of glass, which is generally defined as limiting deflection to the lesser of $L/175$, or 3/4 in. Stone, however, requires more rigid, less deflecting support. Most stone specifications currently limit deflection of the stone supporting elements to the lesser of $L/360$ along the length of the individual stone or 1/8 in., whichever is less. The designer must keep this in mind when adopting previously acceptable aluminum profiles used to support metal and glass panels in new designs supporting stone.

2. Air infiltration is not really a factor in stone versus other panel or cladding materials. The air entry is through joints, not the panel material itself. The size of the individual panels and jointing system, on the other hand, will affect air infiltration. For example, we would expect more air infiltration through a gasketed metal and glass curtain wall than through a caulked stone facade, and more through a caulked stone facade truss/stud support system than through a large precast concrete or glass fiber reinforced concrete panel—it's all a function of joint pattern and joint sealing method. Industry standards allow up to 0.06 cfm/ft^2 of facade area at a pressure differential of 6.24 lb/psf. Our experience, however, has been that the measured air infiltration through truss supported/stone and precast panel facades can approach nil when proper detailing is employed.

3. Water absorption into and penetration through a stone panel is of more concern than through most other panel materials, such as metal and glass. Water can penetrate through "sealed joints" and "perimeter construction" of all panels—not necessarily through the panel itself. In the case of stone, unlike metal and glass and, in general, the denser cementitious materials, it must also be anticipated that water can be absorbed into and will penetrate through the stone itself—through fissures in the stone, as well as by absorption, due to its porous nature. Water deflection, collection, and drainage systems must be designed to

recognize the potential for increased water penetration and the attendant need for control. Stone thickness must be determined not only by the initial strength of the individual dry stone, but also by the possible lessening in strength due to initial water absorption, as well as by the long-term degradation due to repeated freeze/thaw cycles.

4. When designing a metal and glass curtain wall, we need only to evaluate temperature change as the catalyst for expansion and contraction. The same is the case for a metal support system for stone—truss or stud framing, conventional aluminum curtain wall stick or frame systems. Each has its own individual dimension of response to expansion and contraction. For the stone itself, on the other hand, temperature change or the effects of freeze/thaw cycles on the stone itself must be evaluated. Recently, test regimens have been developed by informed design professionals to attempt to determine the long-term degradation of various stones due to the ravages of weather. An ASTM technique used for the evaluation of the effects of freeze/thaw on concrete has been adopted by some design professionals to evaluate the effects of freeze/thaw on the strength and permeability characteristics of stone. The results have been somewhat surprising. While some spalling was to be expected, reduction in modulus of rupture of as much as 20 to 40% was unexpected. Whereas a few years ago, one might have adopted a safety factor of 4 or, in the case of a uniform quality stone, 3, in a stone design based upon the initial qualities of the stone, a 40% reduction in strength due to freeze/thaw over time and not anticipated can effectively reduce the design safety factor to as little as 2.4 and 1.8, respectively, if in service the stone degrades to the extent "predicted" by the test method.

With stone, the selection of material, thickness, and method of support must consider certain environmental conditions in a different light than with a conventional metal and glass facade.

5. All building frames and/or individual components thereof move both vertically and laterally on a continuing basis as a result of the forces impacting upon them. These movements must be accommodated in the relationship of the facade to the frame and in the interrelationship of the components of the facade. The most critical of these requiring attention is the effect of interstory differential floor movement. A stick or unitized curtain wall or stud support system is most severely impacted by interstory differential movement, as such systems are anchored to the building frame at different points of unequal differential floor movement along the building perimeter. A steel truss, precast concrete system, or glass fiber reinforced concrete system, when designed to transfer dead load to the building frame at or near the columns, need not be concerned with the generally large interstory differential building frame movement resulting from live load along the slab or beam edge, but only with the minimal column shortening.

In a typical building frame, which might anticipate no more than 1/8-in. column shortening and as much as 5/8-in. interstory differential vertical movement at center span due to differential live loading, a truss, precast, or glass fiber reinforced concrete system used in a strip window configuration and supported at or near a column need only accommodate 1/8-in. of movement—a 1/4 to 3/8-in. working joint, which can be readily caulked in an aesthetically acceptable manner. On the other hand, an aluminum stick, unitized curtain wall, or stud system supported along the slab or beam edge and using the same building frame characteristics is called upon to accommodate 3/4-in. movement. This could result in a 1 1/2-in. working joint, if we assume a low modulus caulking material. Alternatively, a two-piece head or receptor system can be added at the head of a window to accommodate the anticipated movement; however, this would generally increase the metal band or sightline width and as a gasketed joint contribute to an increase in air infiltration and possible water leakage.

Another alternative which must be considered is the stiffening of the spandrel beam or slab edge to reduce live load interstory differential movement/deflection where joint size and sight lines are critical.

Other considerations which are taken for granted when utilizing metal and glass as facade design elements are uniformity of color and texture, predictability of resistance to breakage during handling, and resistance to discoloration—in other words, staining.

When utilizing stone, precast concrete, or glass fiber reinforced concrete, each must be given different and special consideration.

In metal and glass, reasonable uniformity of color and texture is within the manufacturing control of the contractor. With stone, there is variation from piece to piece, which requires the complete evaluation by a trained eye to determine what will be acceptable under various lighting conditions versus what will be objectionable. While a certain amount of culling can be done during fabrication of the stone as well as during shop-assembled system assembly, the final decision is really made on the building after it is in place and evaluated as an entire facade. Thus, it is essential that the system be designed to facilitate removal and replacement of an offending stone panel or portion thereof. In general, this is most easily accommodated in a glazed-in system. It is more difficult in a pin/drilled-in anchor system, where access is needed to the interior to employ the original anchoring system rather than to accept a face-drilled anchor concealed by a mix of epoxy and stone chips.

The ability to repair or replace an individual stone on the facade is also essential due to the fact that stone is more brittle than other building materials and, as such, more susceptible to cracking during handling and installation. This is particularly important as we use thin stone. Procedures must be at hand to determine whether a particular cracked stone can be satisfactorily repaired or whether it must be replaced. Attention must be addressed to methods of repair and/or replacement during the initial selection and design process. Such considerations are minimal, however, in precast concrete and glass fiber reinforced concrete panels, where bulk resists breakage and repair methods have been proven to withstand the test of time.

The selection of sealant in the past has generally been a function of available sealant color, its colorfastness, and the ability of the sealant to accommodate the anticipated movement. With stone, precast concrete, and glass fiber reinforced concrete, a new ingredient has been added—will the sealant stain the porous materials, thus making the joints appear wider than they really are? Will these porous materials absorb the byproducts of the sealant cure process or the sealant itself, along the bond line, as well as runoff from the sealant surface, creating a visually unacceptable condition? Each stone, precast, or glass fiber reinforced concrete panel formulation under consideration must be tested in conjunction with the specific sealant being considered for use to verify that it will not cause initial or future staining.

Conclusions

No new ground has been covered insofar as new environmental or functional factors to be considered. This was not part of the agenda assigned to me. However, what I have endeavored to show is that the way these conventional factors must be handled does change with the selection of materials and the systems in which they are used. What needs highlighting is the fact that the performance capabilities of individual systems and materials must be determined early on during the design phase. The selection of a particular stone can impact on the support system design, and, conversely, selection of a specific support system has the potential to rule out an individual stone or stone thickness. For example, a thinner or weaker stone can be used more readily in a drilled-in anchor support system, such as a truss, where span between anchors can be controlled without architectural effect, which is not possible in a kerf or glazed-in system, where the stone joint pattern controls anchorage.

The design team must be cautioned not to select a stone type and/or thickness which is not compatible with the designer-preferred support system and joint pattern. Retreating behind the "facade" of a performance specification, while making incompatible prescriptive requirements as to stone type, thickness, and support system, can result in conflict and will be time consuming and costly.

Homework up front, in the form of "precontract" stone evaluation and testing before and during the selection process and prior to issuing possibly incompatible documents, is essential. The design professional has a new regimen to learn when using stone in the modern technologically advanced support systems needed to provide rapidly installed, efficient, and economical building enclosure systems.

Lawrence D. Carbary[1] and William J. Schoenherr[1]

Structural Silicone Sealants Used to Adhere Stone Panels on Exterior Building Facades

REFERENCE: Carbary, L. D. and Schoenherr, W. J., **"Structural Silicone Sealants Used to Adhere Stone Panels on Exterior Building Facades,"** *New Stone Technology, Design, and Construction for Exterior Wall Systems, ASTM STP 996*, B. Donaldson, Ed., American Society for Testing and Materials, Philadelphia, 1988, pp. 160–165.

ABSTRACT: Appropriate design criteria need to be established for this new structural sealant application to ensure curtain wall safety and performance. This paper describes methods of adhering stone panels to a building framework with silicone sealant with emphasis on joint design and special considerations for stone substrates. The paper also explains the testing used to warrant adhesion and compatibility and the application techniques necessary for a quality installation.

KEY WORDS: silicone adhesives on stone, structural attachment with silicone, structural silicone, natural stone, silicone adhesive/sealant

Striking glass facades and curtain walls are visible evidence of how silicone sealant structural glazing has grown in popularity over the past 25 years. Now this technology is expanding to include the use of natural stone panels along with or in place of glass, giving designers greater creative latitude than ever before.

It should be noted that the porous substrates under consideration here are natural stones such as granite and marble. Man-made materials like precast concrete or coated insulating board have low structural integrity and variable surfaces and are not suitable for silicone sealant structural attachment. Furthermore, only silicone sealants have demonstrated, in the laboratory and in the field, the longevity and thermal stability necessary to be used as structural adhesives [1]. Organic sealants are not suitable.

This paper will be illustrated by two construction projects using silicone sealants to structurally attach natural stone panels. The first is the Encino Executive Plaza in Encino, California, with granite attached in much the same manner as many glass structural glazing projects. The second example is 222 Steel Street, Denver, Colorado, utilizing the patented Cygnus Panel System to construct a lightweight curtain wall with a thin veneer of natural stone.

Silicone Sealant Structural Glazing

Structural glazing with silicone sealants dates back over 25 years. These years of testing and actual field experience with various designs using glass have laid a good foundation for the development of sealant structural attaching with stone. There are two structural attachment methods which can be used for either glass or stone. The first is the two-sided method, where two panel edges are held mechanically by a kerf and metal fin support (Fig. 1). The

[1] Dow Corning Corp., Fremont, CA 94537-5121.

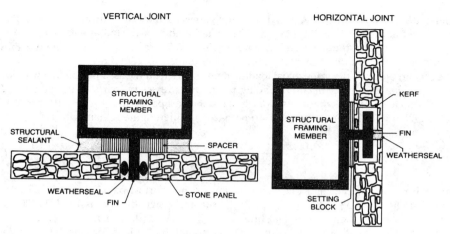

FIG. 1—*Structural stone detail.*

remaining edges are adhered to the framing system with a silicone structural sealant. The other common method for sealant structural attaching is four-sided, where all four panel edges are adhered to the frame with silicone sealant and no frame is visible. This allows the designer to create smooth, uninterrupted facades.

A new, less expensive system of cladding curtain walls with veneers of stone has been developed by Cygnus, Inc. This patented technique for adhering small thin panels of tile to a galvanized metal deck builds on the strengths of silicone sealants and the design experience gained from more traditional sealant structural glazing. Like conventional four-sided structural glazing applications, the sealant bears the weight, or deadload, of the panel. A foam tape functions as a spacer between the stone and metal deck and also acts as a backer rod for applying the weather seal between panels (Fig. 2). Lightweight, highly insulating curtain wall sections can be prefabricated in the shop or factory and fastened mechanically to the building's steel frame at the job site.

Designing Structural Joints

Design standards for structural silicone joints have been established over years of experience with glass. Careful testing, including the use of mock-up joints, has demonstrated that these standards may be applied to stone substrates as well [2]. They deal specifically with calculating the sealant "bite," the area of contact (in square inches) required between sealant and substrate and substrate to support the panel. Structural joints may be subjected to stresses caused by deadload or by wind pulling the panel outwards; also called windload. The sealant bite must be sufficient to retain the panel in the face of these combined forces.

Calculations for sealant bite are based on two theories. The one originally used for sealant structural glazing is the flat plate theory, based on the assumption that panels do not bow out or deflect under windload. This means stress is distributed evenly around the panel perimeter. Here the designer uses the projected windload (W), the measurement of the panel perimeter (P), the panel area (A), and the design strength of the structural sealant (DS) to determine the sealant bite to be specified.

$$\frac{W \times A}{DS \times P} = \text{sealant bite} \tag{1}$$

To illustrate with a real-life example, the granite panels used for the Encino Executive Plaza have a panel perimeter of 6.4 m (252 in.). The wind load is projected at 958 Pa (20 lb/ft²). The design strength of the structural silicone sealant is 137 kPa (20 lb/in.²). Using the above equation, the sealant bite equals 0.00254 m (0.1 in.).

The second theory is the trapezoidal loading theory, based on the assumption that windload stresses will cause panel deflection, leading to greater stresses on parts of the panel [3,4]. The equation based on this theory uses one half the shortest panel side (1/2 SP), the projected windload (W), and the sealant design strength (DS) to determine sealant bite.

$$\frac{(1/2 \ SP \times W)}{DS} = \text{sealant bite} \tag{2}$$

In the Encino example, half the measurement of the shortest panel side is 0.787 m (31 in.), the windload is 958 Pa (20 lb/ft²), and the sealant design strength is 137 kPa (20 psi). Using the above equation, the sealant bite equals 0.00559 m (0.22 in.).

The trapezoidal loading theory is the industry-accepted standard for calculating sealant bite, chiefly because it will always render the more conservative number, designing in an additional safety margin.

In four-sided structural silicone applications, both conventional and thin-veneer, the sealant must bear the deadload of the panel. Deadload may be the critical factor in calculating sealant bite. Dow Corning recommends that sealant bite be calculated to support a maximum deadload of 1 psi. The bite as determined by deadload is then compared to the bite as determined by windload. The more conservative number is then used. This figure represents an extremely conservative insurance factor based on extensive testing.

One final factor should be considered in designing silicone sealant structural joints. Room for caulking must be allowed. Joints should be designed to be at least 1/4 in. thick to allow for a complete sealant "fill." The sealant must achieve good contact with all substrates. A design which makes application or tooling difficult may lead to inadequate contact and adhesion, lowering the structural capabilities of the entire curtain wall.

Thin Veneer Panel Systems

What sets the thin veneer panels system apart from other structural glazing systems is the location of the sealant. In systems of this type the structural sealant is located behind the stone panel, recessed from the edges (Fig. 2). Correct application of the sealant is critical. Sealant is applied in strips on the metal decking, followed immediately by installation of the stone panel by pressing it on top of the sealant. It is important that the sealant strips be thicker than the tape so that when the panel is pressed in place, adequate contact area is achieved. If the spacer tape is too thick or the sealant bead too shallow, the contact area will be too small to supply the strength necessary to adhere the panel.

Special Considerations for Stone Substrates

As pointed out earlier, testing and experience have established that the basic technology of silicone sealant structural glazing is the same for glass or stone panels. The substrates do perform differently, however, and it is worth noting the differences for both design and application purposes.

In some ways, stone substrates have the advantage over other materials used in silicone sealant structural attaching. First of all, they are very rigid, resulting in minimal deflection under wind loading. This reduces the stress of the cleavage force on the sealant caused by

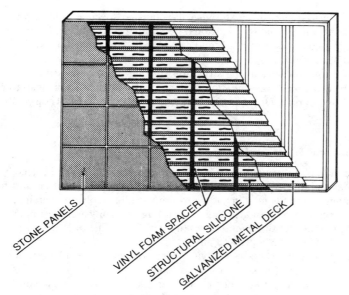

FIG. 2—*Thin veneer panel system.*

the rotation of the panel edge as the center of the panel deflects or bows out under wind loading.

Second, stone substrates like granite or marble typically have a more consistent bonding surface than materials like painted surfaces, coating glasses, or raw metals. This reduces adhesion variability and promotes virtually permanent adhesion.

Third, most stones remain relatively stable in the face of environmental stresses such as extreme temperature and humidity changes. They exhibit a much lower rate of thermal expansion than glass. This reduces the shear force on the sealant during differential thermal expansion.

Besides these advantages, the unique properties of natural stone require careful joint preparation to assure optimal curtain wall performance.

Cleaning of the sealant joint before application is complicated by the relatively rough substrate surface, which can trap dirt from the air or particles and dust created when the panel was cut. If these contaminants are not removed, adhesion can be impaired and the joint will not perform to design.

Sealant Testing

Testing by sealant suppliers plays a major role in establishing the suitability of silicone sealants for structural glazing. As natural stone was introduced to structural glazing, Dow Corning conducted thorough feasibility testing, including the construction of mock-up joints. These were tested under both wet and dry conditions and subjected to accelerated aging. The results affirmed the effectiveness and durability of silicone structural sealants for glazing with stone.

Responsible silicone sealant suppliers also conduct on-going project testing for structural sealant customers. Peel adhesion tests [ASTM Test Method for Adhesion-in-Peel of Elastomeric Joint Sealants (C 794-80)] are conducted with representative job site samples supplied by the customer to make sure materials will adhere as specified and to make general surface preparation recommendations. It should be remembered that field conditions differ from the laboratory, and adhesion tests should be conducted on site to confirm that cleaning and workmanship are satisfactory.

In addition, total compatibility of the structural silicone sealant, substrates, and backup accessories must be confirmed. Incompatibility of accessory materials may lead to adhesion loss or unsightly discoloration. Dow Corning conducts both adhesion and compatibility tests for their customers.

Sealant Application and Workmanship

Silicone structural sealants provide their best performance when applied correctly to clean surfaces. Substrates should be properly cleaned, making sure that all surfaces to be sealed are reached. Cleaning methods may include abrasion cleaning, solvent cleaning, or both.

Abrasion cleaning can be done by grinding, saw cutting, sand or water blasting, mechanical abrading, or a combination of these methods. Any remaining dust or loose particles should be removed by vacuuming or compressed air.

Solvent cleaning is accomplished by applying clean solvent to the substrate with a clean cloth and wiping vigorously. The solvent should then be wiped off with a clean, dry cloth before it evaporates. Adequate time must be allowed for the solvent left in substrate pores to evaporate before applying primer or sealant to insure good adhesion.

At the Encino Executive Plaza, cleaning was accomplished with high pressure hot water. The stone was then allowed to dry indoors for 24 h before sealant application. It should be noted that the appropriateness of this unusual cleaning technique was first confirmed by laboratory adhesion testing conducted by the sealant supplier.

Sealant testing will indicate whether a primer is required. Primers promote adhesion on some substrates, but are not a substitute for cleaning the surface.

It is very important that during application of a sealant or primer, the material not contact adjacent surfaces because these materials are extremely difficult to remove. Contact of sealant or primer on adjacent surfaces may cause discoloration or a change in the appearance of the stone panel during wet rainy weather. Joints where appearance is important must be masked with tape during sealant application to prevent sealant from marring the surface.

Summary

Silicone sealant structural attachment with stone substrates is a viable, attractive system for constructing stone-clad curtain walls. It is based on years of development and experience with glass and a growing number of successful projects in stone.

The beauty and natural attributes of stone, its rigidity and low thermal expansion, make it uniquely suited to silicone sealant structural attachment. This technology has tremendous design potential and represents a growth opportunity for the construction industry. Designers, contractors, and sealant manufacturers working together can help realize the full benefits of this technology.

References

[1] Hilliard, J. R., Parise, C. J., and Peterson, C. O., Jr., "Structural Sealant Glazing," *Sealant Technology in Glazing Systems, ASTM STP 638,* American Society for Testing and Materials, Philadelphia 1977, pp. 67–99.

[2] Internal testing on stone identical to testing on tile, which is documented in International Conference of Building Officials, Report NER 313.

[3] Klosowski, J. and Schmidt, C., "The Role of Adhesive Sealants in Structural Glazing," *U.S. Glass Metal and Glazing,* July/August 1984, pp. 64–70.

[4] Haugsby, M. H., Schoenherr, W. J., Carbary, L. D., and Schmidt, C. M., "Standards for Calculating Structural Silicone Joint Dimensions," to be published by ASTM.

D. Scott Smith[1] and C.O. Peterson, Jr.[1]

The Marriage of Glass and Stone

REFERENCE: Smith, D. S. and Peterson, C. O., Jr., **"The Marriage of Glass and Stone,"** *New Stone Technology, Design, and Construction for Exterior Wall Systems, ASTM STP 966,* B. Donaldson, Ed., American Society for Testing and Materials, Philadelphia, 1988, pp. 166–182.

ABSTRACT: This article reviews two of the many curtain wall systems available to clad the exterior of medium to high rise buildings with glass and stone: the vertical stopless system and the unitized curtain wall system. These glazing methods utilize aluminum as the structural backbone and glass and stone as glazed panels. The systems' major details are individually analyzed and general recommendations on key areas are made, along with a discussion of preliminary design criteria for stone and glass curtain walls. Finally, advantages of both systems are highlighted.

KEY WORDS: granite, curtain wall cladding system, stopless glazing, stone panel, vertical stopless system, unitized wall system, stone glazed curtain walls

The architectural and building communities in the past five to ten years have begun a renewed, revitalized use of natural stone claddings. This trend has inspired engineers, architects, suppliers, fabricators, and contractors to develop new, and enhance existing, methods of cladding structures with natural stone products.

Accompanying this natural stone renaissance has been the move of the architectural communities away from designs of the 1960s and 1970s to the new and innovative creations of the 1980s. Current designs involve the use of new, lighter weight building materials and major technological advances in structural support systems. These trends have helped to pave the way for architectural statements of the 1980s. The new support systems are lightweight, more material efficient, and less expensive than ones previously available to the architectural community. These concepts have been applied to cladding design through the use of thin stone veneer products and thin stone panels which range from 18 to 50 mm thick.

This concept of lightweight support systems for buildings and building skins requires special design techniques that the architect, engineer, general contractor, and subcontractor must all understand and agree upon. The project architect must preestimate the building and floor movements and then specify the deflection limits the cladding system must accommodate while being aware that the larger the building movements, the more costly the cladding system which will successfully accommodate specified building movements.

The design of the curtain wall cladding system should be addressed in the preliminary stages of the building's design. Realistic dead loads from the cladding system must be used in the engineering calculations, which will have a direct impact on the deflection of the floor slabs. The design loads for curtain walls with stone can range from 41 to 100 kg/m², depending on the type of stone, type of glass, the ratio of glass to stone, and height-to-width ratio of each opening. The weight of the spandrel panel varies with the size and thickness of the

[1] PPG Industries, Inc., Pittsburgh, PA 15272.

panel and the stone material chosen. Generally, stone veneer curtain walls today use 25 to 38-mm-thick stone, depending on wind, seismic, and gravity loads. Other important factors affecting the thickness are the stone's physical and mechanical properties.

Types of Curtain Wall Systems with Stone

Details of Vertical Stopless Curtain Wall

The head of the stone/sill of glass detail (Fig. 1) is one of the four basic building block details common to all curtain wall systems using stone in the spandrel areas. Many factors affect the final design of aluminum curtain wall horizontals. One important factor is the weathertight sealing of the stone panels to the horizontals. PPG Industries presently uses only silicone-based caulking to seal the stone to the horizontals. It is important that the correct type of silicone be used for the stone weather seals. Through extensive project mock-up testing, in-house laboratory testing, and a close working relationship with Dow Corning, our company has developed good reliable stone-to-aluminum horizontal weather seals.

The second building block detail is the sill of stone/head of glass detail (Fig. 2). The stone is captured at the sill similar to the head detail; the bite on the stone at the sill should be a minimum of 12 mm. The bite at the head is typically 12 mm but could vary depending on project parameters such as design floor deflection, creep, anticipated thermal movement, etc. The minimum bite must never be less than 6 mm under any conditions to ensure the panel is retained in the opening and to prevent air and water infiltration. The glazing pocket size will vary according to the parameters and requirements of the architectural specifications and the required thickness of the stone panels to maintain minimum field proven clearances between the horizontal and stone panel.

VERTICAL STOPLESS SYSTEM DETAILS

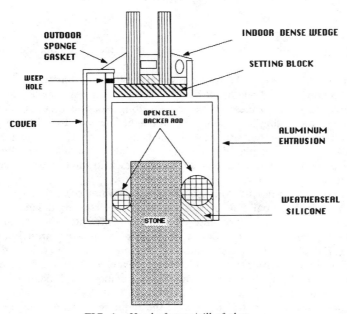

FIG. 1—*Head of stone/sill of glass.*

VERTICAL STOPLESS SYSTEM DETAILS

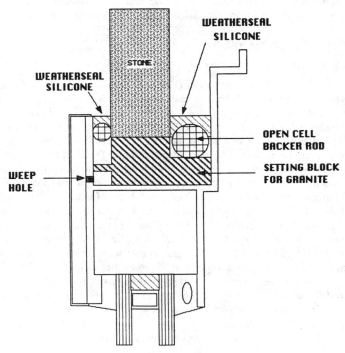

FIG. 2—*Sill of stone/head of glass.*

Our company recommends four important concepts in the sill of stone/head of glass detail:

1. The sill of the stone must be weeped with a minimum of one 9.5-mm-diameter weep hole per 1.525 m width of stone panel based on field testing experience.

2. The recommended hardness for the stone setting blocks is 80 to 90 durometer shore A. The height of the setting block should be sufficient to ensure that the edges of the stone do not bear on the framing system; the minimum height must not be less than 3 mm. Ideally, the setting blocks should be placed at the quarter points but should never be placed closer than 15.2 cm from the nearest edge of the setting block to the corners of the stone panel without an engineering review.

3. Our company recommends the use of a backup water collection system behind the stone panel to protect the building interior (Fig. 2). This secondary defensive system should be designed to gather condensation and water that has infiltrated through the panel or the framing system. The water is then drained outdoors via tubes or through a well-designed weep system. Each backup water collection system must be custom designed for each particular project. Project parameters that affect the water collection system design include porosity and finish of stone, regional climactic environment, and location of insulation in the stone spandrel area.

4. The stone must be shimmed to provide the required horizontal edge clearance until the silicone sealant has cured. The temporary shims are then removed and the voids filled with silicone sealant.

The vertical mullion is involved in two of the four basic details of the vertical stopless system. The section taken through the vertical I beam mullion (or tubular mullion not shown) at the vision glass area (Fig. 3) is an extremely important detail since it provides the structural backbone for this type of curtain wall system. The glass is adhered with structural silicone to a vertical adapter which is attached to the vertical mullion. The wind load is then transferred to the vertical mullion and to the building through the floor anchors. The vertical mullion section through the stone-to-stone vertical joint can be seen in Fig. 4. The stone spandrel panel may or may not require structural silicone attachment to the vertical mullion; this depends on the strength of the stone, the thickness of the stone, and the design specifications. The horizontals are attached to vertical mullions and transfer the wind and gravity loads to the vertical mullions. The minimum design width for the stone-to-stone caulking joint should not be less than 12 mm. The caulking must be designed to accommodate for stone tolerances, maintain minimum seal widths, and allow for ease of erection.

There are three other details which are typical to many of PPGs stone-curtain wall projects. They are: (a) stone setting flush onto the floor; (b) a stone-to-stone outside 90° corner; and (c) stone-to-stone joint with no exposed metal.

Figure 5 shows how PPG has typically set a sill to a floor or a curb. A kerf cut in the stone accepts the anchor, which should be a nonferrous material, typically aluminum or

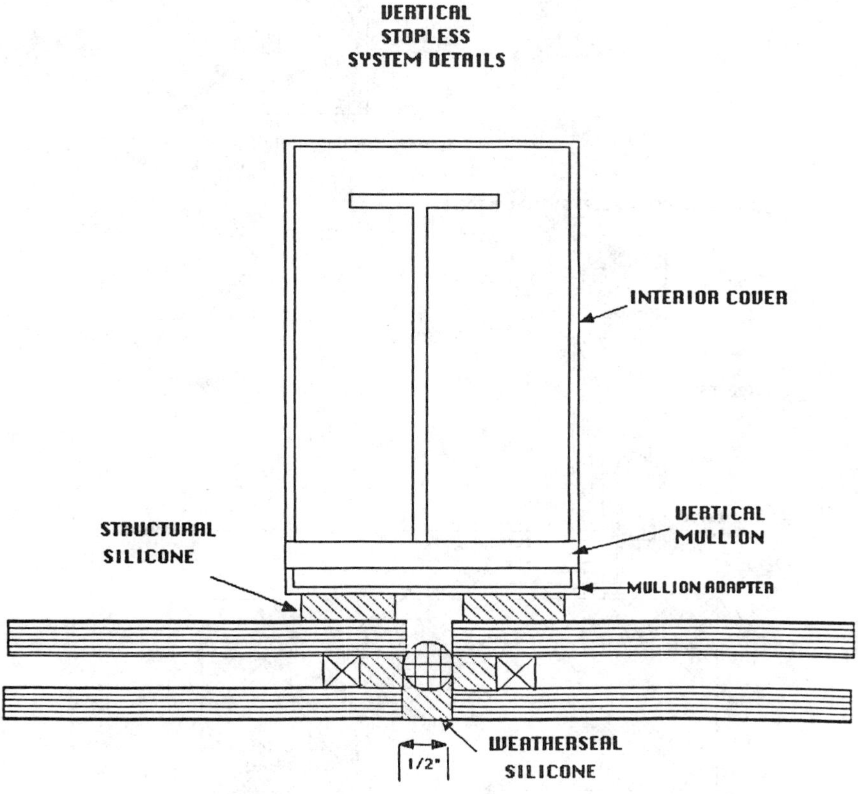

FIG. 3—*Typical vertical mullion at vision glass.*

VERTICAL STOPLESS SYSTEM DETAILS

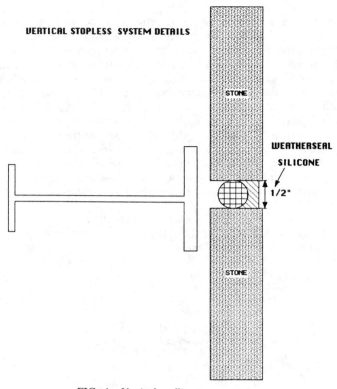

FIG. 4—*Vertical mullion at stone joint.*

VERTICAL STOPLESS SYSTEM DETAILS

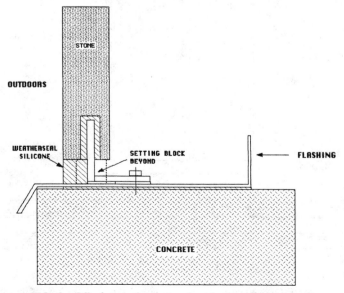

FIG. 5—*Sill of stone detail at curb or bottom of curtain wall.*

VERTICAL STOPLESS SYSTEM DETAILS

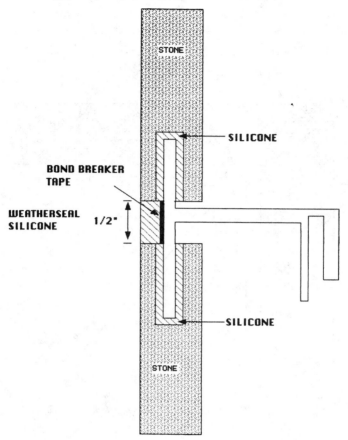

FIG. 6—*Typical granite-to-granite joint.*

stainless steel. The stone is set on setting blocks, and silicone sealant is applied to form a weather seal; a weep/flashing system is required to drain any water to the outdoors; weep tubes must be used to allow for proper weepage.

The stone-to-stone joint is typically used at the parapet of the building or near the balcony areas. This detail (Fig. 6) allows for the stone to be set without outdoor metal exposed. Three key recommendations must be followed when considering this setting detail. To avoid three-side adhesion, bond breaker tape must be applied to the aluminum horizontal. The stone must be set on setting blocks and sealed with silicone. Setting blocks are usually a silicone or silicone-compatible material as verified by the silicone manufacturer. Curtain wall movements must be limited to a maximum of 6 mm in areas using this detail.

Figure 7 illustrates an outside 90° corner. The stone is cut at a 45° quirk miter joint. The joint must be a minimum of 12 mm wide, and correct caulking and tooling of the silicone weather seal is essential.

Details for the Unitized Wall System

Unitized curtain wall details vary significantly depending on architectural specifications, design parameters, and climatic environment. Unitized wall systems are chiefly characterized

VERTICAL STOPLESS SYSTEM DETAILS

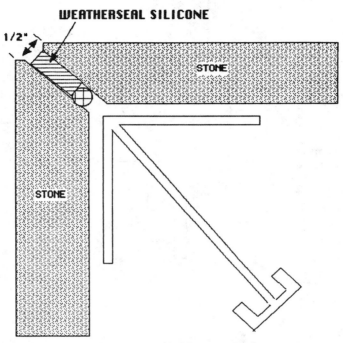

FIG. 7—*Outside 90° corner detail.*

by shop glazing of glass and stone into a prefabricated aluminum framing system. The size of the "typical unit" (Fig. 8) is governed by the project's aesthetic design, shipping limitations, and material availability.

The head of stone/sill of glass (Fig. 9) shows a stack or erection joint in a unitized stone glazed curtain wall. Figure 9 shows the glass and stone offset; this is one of many aesthetic effects achievable using unitized curtain wall cladding systems. The stone is structurally silicone adhered to the horizontal head of the lower unit and is also kerfed to provide an additional retention system. The glass is typically adhered to the sill with structural silicone and allowed to cure.

The neoprene weather strips, illustrated in Fig. 9, prevent water and air from entering the building through the moving stack joint. The joints' movement capability can be designed to accommodate a range of specified building movements.

Figure 10, the sill of stone/head glass, illustrates an attachment concept for the base of the stone. The stone is adhered to the framing system with structural silicone and is mechanically anchored in a kerf which provides attachment. A secondary water defense system is provided through the use of a gutter system which is sealed to the vertical mullion. A weep hole is drilled in the vertical mullion to allow the water to flow from the drainage gutter to the outdoors. Figure 11 illustrates a stone-to-stone horizontal using a combination

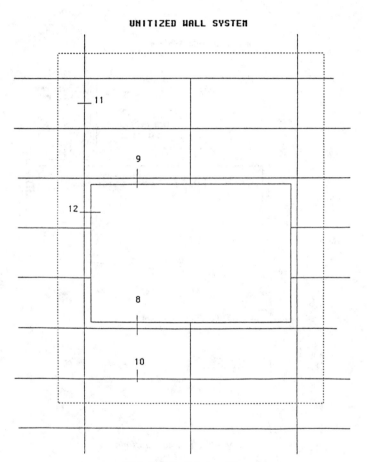

FIG. 8—*Partial elevation.*

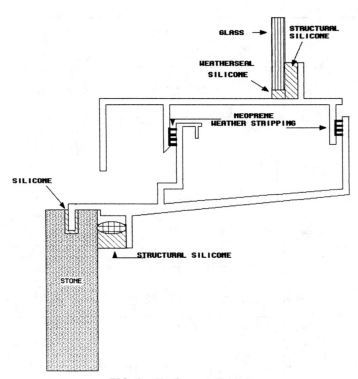

FIG. 9—*Head stone/sill of glass.*

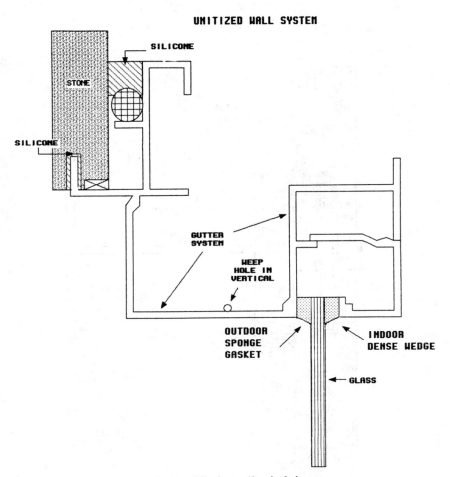

FIG. 10—*Sill of stone/head of glass.*

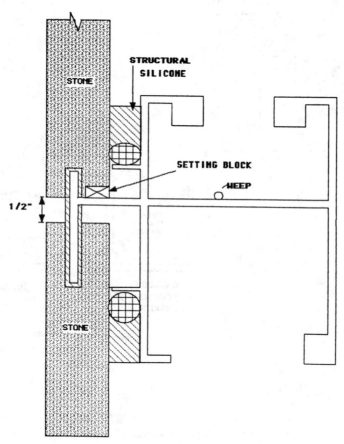

FIG. 11—*Stone-to-stone horizontal joint.*

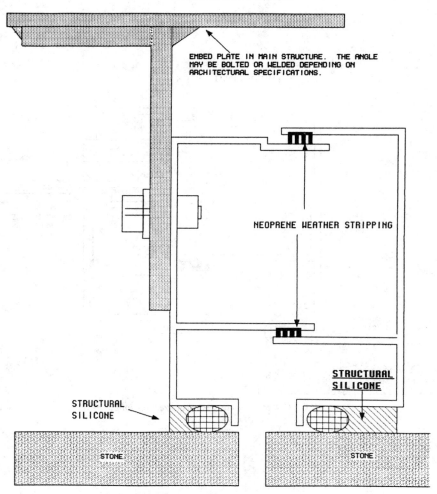

FIG. 12—*Vertical stone-to-stone erection joint.*

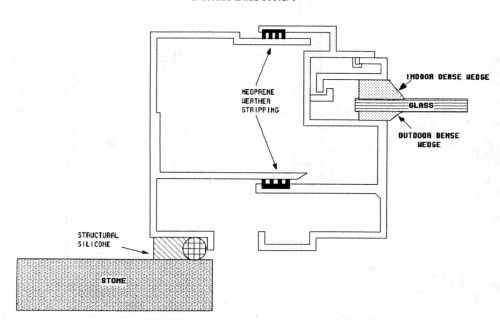

FIG. 13—*Stone-to-glass vertical erection joint.*

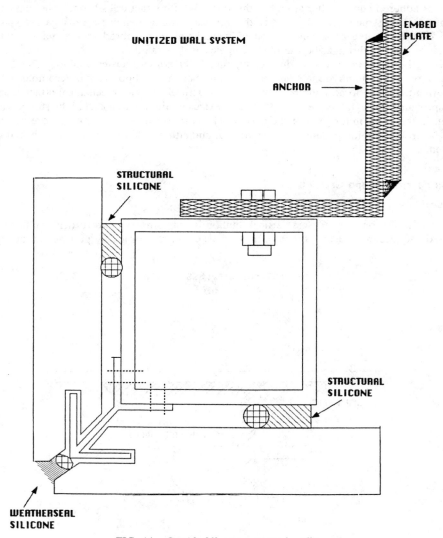

FIG. 14—*Outside 90° corner vertical mullion.*

of structural silicone and anchor attachment. Any water infiltration or condensation may be drained to the outdoors through the weep holes in the vertical framing members (jambs).

Vertical erection joints, (Figs. 12 and 13) are similar in concept to a horizontal stack or erection joint. Neoprene weather stripping is used to prevent air and water infiltration. The stone is adhered and weather sealed to the verticals with structural silicone. The glass may or may not be structurally siliconed to the vertical framing members; a dry gasket system may be used in lieu of silicone. Each individual unit is anchored to the main building structure, usually through the use of steel angles as illustrated in Fig. 12.

Figure 14 illustrates a section through an outside 90° corner, vertical mullion. The corner unit is formed by joining one stone panel to another in the shop. This is accomplished by adhering the stone to an aluminum tube with structural silicone; mechanical attachment is also provided through the use of an aluminum extrusion fitted into a kerf in the stone, which is cut in the quirk miter joint at the corner. The corner is allowed to cure before moving. The horizontal retaining members are miter cut and either welded and sealed or spliced and sealed.

Shop Fabrication and Erection

Vertical Stopless System

Shop fabrication of a stopless vertical mullion is not complex. The vertical mullions are slotted and drilled to receive the floor anchors (see Fig. 15). Holes are punched in the front

VERTICAL STOPLESS SYSTEM

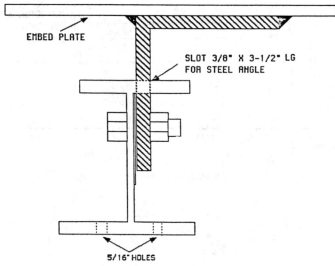

EMBED PLATE

SLOT 3/8" X 3-1/2" LG
FOR STEEL ANGLE

5/16" HOLES

FIG. 15—*Typical anchor detail.*

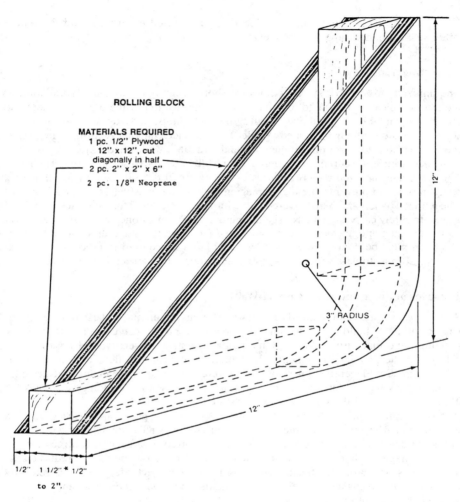

ROLLING BLOCK

MATERIALS REQUIRED
1 pc. 1/2" Plywood
12" x 12", cut
diagonally in half
2 pc. 2" x 2" x 6"

2 pc. 1/8" Neoprene

12"

3" RADIUS

12"

1/2"   1 1/2" * 1/2"

to 2".

*Varies with thickness of stone

FIG. 16—*Rolling block.*

face of the mullions to attach horizontals. The horizontals are cut to size, and properly located weep holes are drilled. The framing system's components are then properly tagged and shipped to the job site for erection. All pieces are shipped loose and assembled at the job site.

Upon receiving the aluminum extrusions, the physical erection of components begins. The vertical mullions (Fig. 15) are erected, and then the horizontals are bolted to the vertical mullions. The building at this point may appear as a town jail or an old type correctional center. The positioning of the stone and glass prior to glazing is accomplished through the use of a turning block or other mechanical devices (Fig. 16). As glass and stone are glazed into the rectangular openings created by the aluminum extrusions (see Figs. 2 and 3), the architect's creation begins to take shape. The structural caulking (see Fig. 3) is applied and allowed to cure. The indoor trim is attached to the erected extrusions, and the outdoor weather seal caulking is applied one elevation at a time.

Unitized Wall System

The unitized curtain wall system allows for shop assembly of the glass, aluminum, and stone into a typical unit prior to job site delivery. Fabrication of the aluminum extrusions is the first step in fabricating a unitized wall system. The fabricated extrusions are assembled, and all concealed caulking is applied. While the concealed caulking is curing, the glass and stone are glazed into appropriate openings and structurally siliconed. After the structural silicone has sufficiently cured, the panels are carefully moved to a storage area. The moving of the assembled unitized panels requires extreme care both in the shop as well as at the job site in order to prevent potential damaging racking and twisting of the glazed units.

The unitized panels are then delivered to the job site on modified flat bed trucks specifically designed to safely carry the panels. The aluminum, glass, and stone panels are then hoisted onto the building and are permanently anchored (see Fig. 12). Field erection of a unitized wall system must be done sequentially; less field labor is required to erect a unitized wall as compared to a stopless vertical system because more shop assembly is achievable.

Advantages of Stone and Glass Curtain Walls

The vertical stopless and unitized curtain wall systems are unique and exciting design tools for the cladding of buildings with stone. This design approach can cost-effectively be used on medium and high rise buildings. One major advantage of this type of approach is its ability to handle building movements, particularly buildings with floor deflections greater than ±6 mm. Cantilevered floor slabs, cantilevered corners, and column spacing greater than 6.1 m may be problems for some types of traditional stone cladding systems but are not a burden to a well-designed curtain wall system.

The stone can be glazed flush or offset with respect to the glass; stone glazed soffits are also available. The erection of the stone glazed curtain wall system by a single erector reduces the amount of construction coordination required by a general contractor or construction manager. Other advantages include warranties from a single source, reduced scheduling activities, and easier administration of contracts and project safety. Stone glazed curtain walls offer architects, owners, developers, and building managers definite advantages ranging from aesthetic appeal to warranties.

Subject Index

Author Index